How NOT To Buy A Common Stock

How NOT To Buy

A Common Stock

by DONALD I. ROGERS

ARLINGTON HOUSE

New Rochelle   New York

Library of Congress Catalog Card Number: 70-183678

ISBN 0-87000-145-0

MANUFACTURED IN THE UNITED STATES OF AMERICA

TO

David D. Rogers

AND

Nancy E. Rogers

Contents

1 *The Legacy*

When Sam Webster's Aunt Martha went to her Great Reward at age ninety, there was about seventeen thousand dollars in cash left in her estate. Of her once-numerous progeny, only Sam remained. By the time her small bills had been settled up, Sam learned that he was to receive an undisputed legacy of about fifteen thousand dollars.

He was overwhelmed.

It was exactly as much as he earned by working hard all year. Here he was with a full year's pay in his pocket, so to speak, and for the first time in his life he felt truly secure and independent.

It was then that Sam began making a long series of mistakes that are common to many small investors.

Long before Aunt Martha's check arrived, there were numerous family conferences. First off, he was to get the new eyeglasses that he needed but that were budgeted for three months hence. His wife, Adele, was to have her dental work done immediately, instead of after the first of the year as the old budgetary plans had decreed. Randy would not have to wait until his birthday for his much-needed bicycle, and Lisa could have the stereo set for her room if she contributed the thirty dollars that she had already saved toward it from her earnings as a baby-sitter.

Some nagging bills would be paid.

About fourteen thousand dollars would remain.

About four thousand dollars would go into a savings account, the Websters decided, preferably one of those long-term two-year accounts that draw the maximum amount of interest. Why not long-term? After all, Sam was still earning a good week's pay.

The remaining ten thousand would go into good common

stocks and, with any kind of luck, the nest-egg would be greatly enlarged within the year.

Sam pointed out that conditions for investing were just right. The market had been good for several months and gains were posted on common stock prices almost every day. Corporate earnings were high. Profits were making records in many industries. The economy was strong. Prosperity smiled on the land. Employment was rising; unemployment was dropping.

All in all, Sam said, it was an ideal time to buy common stocks.

Sam had never bought any stock before so the first thing he did was to buy a few popular books on how to invest, and he had Adele read them, too. This produced many lively discussions around the Webster house as he and Adele combed through the stock lists and debated the merits of one company or another.

They sent for the annual reports of those companies that seemed to offer the most likely prospects for investment, and studied them carefully, looking at the profit picture and the cash position as revealed by the financial statements.

They wanted to consult with a good broker about the companies that seemed attractive to them, but they didn't know which broker to pick. Several advertised in the financial section of their local newspaper. The yellow pages of the phone directory revealed that there were a large number of brokers in their town, all with names that sounded legal, regal or pompous.

"I suppose," Sam told Adele, "that they're something like banks: one is as good as another until you want an extra loan or you create an overdraft, then they're all equally bad."

"I guess you're right," Adele replied, "but speaking of banks, why not ask our banker whom *he* would recommend?"

"Good idea," Sam said. "He certainly ought to know the name of the best broker."

So next day Sam stopped by to see Mr. Connolly at the bank.

"Well, *I* don't want to recommend a broker," the banker said. "Suppose the man you deal with turns out to be a bum. Then you'll blame me."

"Oh, no, I wouldn't," Sam assured him. "I realize that we're dealing with human beings here, and there's always the possibility that one may not turn out as you expect."

"Why don't you put your money into one of our thrift accounts?" Mr. Connolly asked. "And we could put some in a Certificate of Deposit that would pay you a guaranteed high rate of interest. It's a sort of short-term bond."

"I've already got a good savings account. I want to put this into some solid common stocks. I should be in this market now, taking advantage of it."

"Well," Mr. Connolly said, "suppose I give you the names of three brokers whom I can recommend as being solid and in good standing in the community, and then you can make your own choice."

"You're using the same technique a hospital does in recommending a doctor," Sam said. "It's a way of avoiding responsibility."

"It's the only way to be fair," Mr. Connolly rejoined, implying that "being fair" is a basic banking function that is monitored by the Federal Reserve Board.

He then drew a memo pad toward him and wrote down the names of three brokerage firms. Handing the sheet of paper to Sam he said, "This is the best I can do for you, Mr. Webster."

Sam and Adele debated the names on the list briefly, then decided on the one that sounded good to their ears when they repeated it aloud. It had an old-school ring to it, implying not only stability and conservatism, but solid professionalism, with an inside edge on things financial. It rolled off the tongue well.

Sam called the firm and stated that he wanted to invest some money in the stock market. His call was immediately transferred to a man who announced he would take his order.

"I have no order to give," Sam said. "I want to invest some money and I'd like to talk to someone about it."

"Do you have an account here, sir?" asked the man.

"Account? Do I have to have an account? No, I haven't got an account. I guess I'll have to open one."

"Yes, sir. Let me transfer you to our Mr. Poole—that's with a final "e," sir—and he'll help you."

Sam talked briefly to Mr. Poole whose basic concern, it seemed, was whether Sam wanted to trade on margin. When Sam said that he mostly wanted to invest in some good growth stocks, and for cash, Mr. Poole told him he would send him some forms to fill out and return.

Two days later there arrived in the mail some printed records to be filled out in duplicate, and to Sam it seemed very much as though he were making a credit application. The information required included his Social Security number, his address and previous address, his business affiliation with address and telephone number, his banking references, and the names of the members of his immediate family.

He hand-printed the required information (as requested) and mailed it back to the broker. Two days later a man from the firm named Mr. George Fosborg called him at the office and asked for an appointment. When Sam said he was booked solid for the next day or so, Mr. Fosborg invited him to lunch at one of the fine, well-known restaurants near the financial district. Sam accepted with pleasure, feeling he was being welcomed into a new and affluent fraternity.

Mr. Fosborg was a handsome easy-mannered man, impeccably dressed, who made Sam feel at ease and most welcome. They were ushered to a splendid corner table beside one of the broad windows that commanded a view of the city's classic skyline.

After the second martini, Sam stated his needs.

"I have ten thousand dollars to invest," he said, "and I need some guidance and counsel."

"Do you have any particular stock in mind?"

"I have some stocks in mind, but I don't know whether they're any good or not, and I'm not sure I know how to tell the difference between a good stock and a bad one. I'm new at this. What I think I need more than anything else is a well-balanced portfolio."

"Well, you can't hope for complete balance in a portfolio of only ten thousand dollars."

"Hopefully it won't be that size for too long," Sam said. "Maybe we can increase that basic package so that it's easier to manage."

"Yes, I certainly hope so. Now, just what stocks did you have in mind, Sam—you don't mind if I call you Sam?"

"Not at all." Sam named three corporations that had attracted their attention when he and Adele had checked out the earnings reports.

"One of them is a stock that our firm is recommending at the present time," Mr. Fosborg said, naming it. "The other two, I don't know about. I'll have to check with our research department and see what the people there think about them."

"You see what I'm after," Sam explained. "One of these is a utility, the other an electronics space-age company, the third is a conglomerate that operates in many fields. This would give me diversity."

"To some extent—to some extent," Mr. Fosborg replied. "There may be better things in a portfolio than diversity. Quick growth, for instance."

"Of course."

"Suppose we work up something for you and I'll get back to you in a couple of days."

"All right. You'll let me know before you do any buying?"

"Oh, yes. I couldn't buy unless it's on your specific order."

"Fine."

The meal ended pleasantly. Mr. Fosborg left with his assignment and Sam returned to his office filled with good food and drink and glowing high hopes.

Mr. Fosborg called the next day and made an apoointment to see Sam at his office at the beginning of the week, promising to have all of the facts and figures ready for presentation.

"Remember," Sam warned, "I'm looking for some good medium-priced stock with exceptional growth potential." He seemed to have forgotten about diversity.

"That's what I'll try to recommend for you—that, plus some kind of diversity," Mr. Fosborg pledged.

Over the weekend Sam and Adele could feel the excitement growing in them as they anticipated what Mr. Fosborg would prepare for their new portfolio.

"It's like expecting a new baby, or maybe like starting out on a new career," Sam told Adele, glancing up from his copy of the *Wall Street Journal*.

"In a way it's both," Adele replied. "It may be a new career for you—and it may mean the start of a new life for both of us."

"You think I really *could* make enough money in the market to retire from my job and take up investing as a career?"

"I suppose it is done by others," Adele said. "It certainly would be nice to have you working out of our home and not going off to the office every day."

Adele decided to join Sam at his office Monday morning for the meeting with Mr. Fosborg. She wanted to be there at the unveiling of this thrilling milestone in their lives.

Mr. Fosborg had his recommendations all typed up and inserted in a folder with a legal-looking blue jacket on it and their names, "MR. AND MRS. SAMUEL WEBSTER," in gold lettering on the cover. He consulted a small leather notebook as he explained to them why the selections had been made.

The most important recommendation was a major blue-chip company whose stock sold at over one hundred dollars a share, and the provision for purchase of fifty shares used up more than half the funds the Websters had available. This, Mr. Fosborg explained, was the "backbone" of the portfolio and it would be increased from time to time if all went well. The company had an impressive dividend record and its recent sales and profits were pleasing. He cited those figures for his clients.

The next recommendation was for fifty shares of the stock that Sam had wanted—the one that Mr. Fosborg's firm also recommended.

He said that Sam had shown good judgment in picking that one and the research department and the market analyst had both confirmed it as a good choice.

Then there was one hundred shares of what Mr. Fosborg called a *penny stock*. It was cheap, he said, and speculative, but many thought that the corporation had a fair chance to succeed in a big way. It was in the business of supplying hardware to the computer industry and it might make a big profit showing. This item in the portfolio would provide a little "spice," Mr. Fosborg said, and give Sam a run for his money. If he lost, he wouldn't lose too much, and if he won, he could win in a big way. Sam and Adele nodded, pleased with his perception of their needs.

The final item was for twenty-five shares of a conglomerate corporation, one that had sprawled into many fields. It was not the particular conglomerate that Sam had recommended for consideration, but it was a well-known firm that had once been a major appliance manufacturer.

This, Mr. Fosborg explained, rounded out the portfolio and provided the right amount of balance.

When it was all totaled, it came to more than eleven thousand dollars plus commissions, but after a hurried consultation during which Mr. Fosborg discreetly left the office, Sam and Adele decided to reduce their savings account by the required amount and go ahead with Mr. Fosborg's suggestions.

When, they asked, could they actually get the stock?

"All I have to do is call my office," Mr. Fosborg said, "and with your authorization, I'll give the orders now, and they'll be executed by our man on the Stock Exchange floor just as soon as possible— probably within a few minutes. The stock certificates themselves will come from the various stock transfer companies to our firm, and they'll be sent along to you within a few days."

"Well, then, go ahead," said Sam, feeling like the mayor when he pressed the button to open the new bridge.

"Yes, please do," Adele added.

"You will notice," Mr. Fosborg said, "that I will quote the price at which you wish to buy these shares. If I didn't do that it would mean that you would be buying "at market," and in the event that prices are trading higher today, you'd have to pay more for your shares. This way, if the stock can't be bought at our price, the order won't be executed until the trading price matches the one we have quoted."

"That's fine. Just fine."

Mr. Fosborg made his call. The orders were repeated back to him and he repeated them to Sam and Adele. The receipt of the orders was confirmed by the firm's order department.

Adele got up from her chair at the side of the desk and gave Sam a resounding kiss.

Sam leaned back in his swivel chair and smiled.

"Well, sir," Mr. Fosborg said, "you're now a stockholder in four thriving American corporations. Congratulations!"

"Thank you," Sam said. "And now that it's nearly lunchtime and we have my beautiful wife in tow, why not let *me* do the honors this time at *my* favorite restaurant."

Sam and Adele left the office hand in hand, mighty proud of themselves. They were now active part-owners of a good cross-section of the giant American industrial and commercial complex.

They were, they thought, using their legacy prudently.

BUT—

Despite their careful preparations, Sam and Adele had made *fifteen* basic mistakes getting started as investors in the stock market.

If you can re-read this chapter and identify those serious errors, this book is not for you.

II *What Sam Did Wrong*

To Sam and Adele Webster it seemed that a bright new world had opened to them. Its foundation was firmly based on security—self-made security (with an assist from old Aunt Martha)—that would endure no matter what happened to the economy or what foibles of men or committees beset the corporate world. Sam, as the cliche goes, "had it made," or so he thought. Intimate friends of the Websters who learned of their good fortune shared the belief that the couple would have no further worries.

Sam counted his blessings. There was no longer reason for him to fear losing his job. He held a responsible position and did his work well. He was not in a salary bracket that would cause his superiors in the large corporation to look for ways to ease him out, for reasons of envy or economy. In the event of illness he had his company-paid hospitalization plan. In the unlikely event of his death, he had a fine insurance policy.

For the first time in years he felt absolutely free of tension and his attitude was reflected on the job where his superiors told him he was doing better work than ever and complimented him on his results.

Sam and Adele found new dimensions of happiness, and it was traceable to the security offered by Sam's portfolio of stocks.

No one, least of all the Websters, seemed to realize that Sam had made some grievous and potentially costly errors that could jeopardize the continued existence of Aunt Martha's legacy.

He had created, with a series of blunders, a classic case of how *not* to buy common stock. Sam Webster's poor performance is repeated to some extent countless times each day throughout America and the Western world.

It is repeated by those who don't succeed in the stock market, and who wonder why they don't.

They are the losers, and they outnumber the winners by a wide margin.

Of Sam's fifteen glaring errors, two involved mistakes in personal money management. Thirteen were basic errors in dealing with the stock market.

Here, step-by-step, are Sam's goofs:

1. He started out with the wrong ratio of savings-to-investments for a man of modest means. He should have put at least half of his legacy into savings until he found out, from experience, just how much *liquidity* he and his family would need. In common with most of us he had been living to the full extent of his salary—and sometimes a little beyond—hoping one day to build up a cushion of savings. Now he had it, but he didn't know what size cushion fit his needs. It would have been better to have one too large than to cut it, irreparably, too small.

2. He erred in setting up his savings account on a long-term basis, committing his cash for a specified length of time. A savings account should provide the saver with *quick assets* or liquidity—cash on which he can lay his hands on short notice. His account doesn't provide for that.

At least half of his savings should have gone into a thrift, or day-of-deposit–day-of-withdrawal account, to provide for the ready accessibility of cash that might be needed in some emergency or other. As it is, if he needs money he'll have to take out a passbook loan—that is, he'll be borrowing his own money back from the bank and paying interest on it.

3. Sam thought that conditions for investing were just right, and pointed to the fine record of the market in the last few months. Actually he was planning to enter at the top of the market, when most prices were high. Conditions were not just right at all. It was not a good time to buy. Instead, it was a time for careful selectivity

in buying stocks—a time, in fact, for skilled professionals only.

4. Reading the stock lists and thumbing through annual reports of companies can be enlightening to the trained observer, but the exercise is not likely to give you clues as to what to buy in the market. There are many other ways to sniff out the scent of a good stock, as we shall explain in detail, but, for an opener, simply reading the financial and business *news* is more valuable than reading the statistics. The reports of market researchers and analysts, readily available to the public, furnish the rudimentary equipment for getting started on your own research.

5. Your banker is not the person to recommend a broker. Adele gave some poor advice to Sam in this respect and it is too bad he followed it.

A banker's contact with a brokerage firm is on a different level than an individual's. The banker buys and sells only bonds and preferred stocks or common stocks so "gilt-edged" that they can only be described as "deep blue." Any other relationship with the broker may be limited to the financing of margin accounts by issuing brokers' loans, which are referred to as *call money*. This is a world of much higher financial sophistication than Sam required, and a broker who may be fine for a banker may be incompetent when it comes to handling small accounts.

6. Sam, nevertheless, shouldn't have ignored the advice of his banker to invest in a thrift account as well as a Certificate of Deposit. A "CD" is nothing more than a long-term savings account—a sort of non-negotiable bond with a specific interest rate. The rate is higher than the ordinary savings account rate.

7. There are more practical ways to select a broker, as we will show, but the best way is to sample his wares—simply ask him what he can do for you, and judge him by what he recommends. Brokerage house names are likely to seem theatrically pompous, not as a calculated thing to trick the uninitiated, but simply because it's part of the Wall Street syndrome. Alas, Sam forgot that, "A rose by any other name . . ."

8. Sam's entire approach to the representative of the brokerage firm was wrong, for it deprived him of the most valuable service the broker could offer—advice. He should not have stated categorically that he wanted to open an account. He should have let the broker try to persuade him to do business with some well-considered recommendations, that he could compare with the recommendations of other brokers.

9. Sam should not have revealed that he had some specific stocks in mind. He was no expert, and neither was Fosborg. He should have realized that Fosborg was a salesman for the firm, not an analyst or a researcher. As a salesman, Fosborg was handed a fine tip, so that he knew just what area of investment would most interest Sam. Sam should have let Fosborg initiate any suggestions or recommendations.

By his revelations, Sam informed the firm that he was a complete novice. As a result, he may not have received the maximum in time and effort when his portfolio was under consideration.

10. Sam believed Fosborg when he said you can't have complete balance in a portfolio worth only ten thousand dollars.

Like hell you can't. You can have a tightly balanced portfolio for half that amount.

Salesmen, who live on their commissions, like to keep a portfolio open and active so that there is much trading in it—in and out sales and switching from one stock to another. This may or may not be a good thing to do. It all depends on the stocks and the market at the time. But one thing is certain—it's no way to start out, as Sam was doing.

11. Sam assumed that the analysis and research departments of his brokerage firm would automatically go to work in his behalf. Not true. They will only respond to specific assignments, and when Sam stated that he wanted a utility, a space age stock and a conglomerate, he simply set himself up for an unresearched tailor-made pitch.

There will come a time in Sam's life when he will call his broker and order a specific stock by name and set a price that he is willing to pay for it. He was certainly in no position to take such initiative when he had lunch with Fosborg. He'll do that when he's more of an expert. Listing the categories of stocks he wanted in his portfolio was about as sensible as telling a doctor what kind of medicine you want for a complaint that has brought you to his office.

12. Why should Sam have believed Fosborg when he said there were "better things than diversity" for his portfolio? It's a meaningless expression. For a man starting out with a small portfolio, balance is a most desirable goal, and balance is achieved through diversity. If one industry is depressed, another might not be. Actually, through sheer luck, Sam had selected a utility along with his other common stocks. It was a wise choice, for on many occasions, utilities have held the line when other common stocks were depressed. Conversely, there have been times when utilities were down a bit when other stocks were gaining, due to switching from the "safer" utilities to more speculative performers.

A portfolio without some sort of technical balance is better suited for a man of considerable means, one who plans to do a fair amount of trading and who can afford to take a loss now and again if his choices have been wrong. Much depends on the man's tax bracket in such a situation—and Sam's doesn't yet qualify him for much of a tax loss.

13. Sam should have protested the plan to use up half of his available money buying one expensive blue-chip stock. If a blue chip was deemed essential by the man who prepared the portfolio—perhaps to add strength to it—there are many that are available in a much lower price field.

If Sam were to buy a lower priced stock, he would be better able to buy one hundred shares. When stock is sold in lots of one hundred shares it is called a *block*. When it is sold in lots that are less than one hundred shares, it is called an *odd lot deal* and the buyer has to pay an additional commission to the broker. That's because no sales are made at the Stock Exchange unless they are in a *block*, so the broker has to buy the *block* anyway. If the buyer orders only sixty

shares, for instance, the broker is left with forty shares on his hands
that he must dispose of as best he can. This entails extra time and
effort, so an added cost—a percentage of the sale price—is levied
against the buyer.

14. There is no need to buy stock "blind." Sam really made no
selection and exercised no judgment. With the other two recommendations, Mr. Fosborg pushed the stocks that his firm wanted to
sell. There is the possibility that the firm had taken *positions* in these
stocks. Brokerage firms normally do not maintain inventories of
stocks, but buy them on order from their customers. Occasionally,
however, they will *take a position* in a security in the belief that it
will increase in price if they succeed in promoting it to the public.

Chances are, though, that no one at the brokerage firm exercised much judgment on Sam's account, but merely filled in the
recommendations that he had indicated he wanted. Sam should
have asked for the name of the person who recommended the stocks,
and should have read his report on them to see *why* he made the
recommendations.

Analysts, for the most part, don't like to fool themselves or their
firms, and are usually quite candid in their reports. They state what
they don't like about a company or its stock just as frequently as they
list the things they like. Sam might have been surprised at what he
read. Surely he would have been a more enlightened and wiser
investor. It would have done him no harm to have Fosborg work a
little harder for his commission.

15. Naive and gullible, Sam snapped like a hungry fish at a fat
worm when presented with Mr. Fosborg's explanation of buying *at
market.* Fosborg told him, you'll recall, that he was quoting a price
for the stocks to indicate that this was the price Sam was willing to
pay, and if prices had moved higher during the trading session that
day, the order wouldn't be executed.

There's another side to that coin, of course, but Sam never
flipped it over to look at it. What if prices, that morning, had turned
lower? If they had, Sam was putting in a bid for a higher-than-
market price. He was *supporting* the prices, and if any had sagged

during the morning session, he was pulling them back up there with his generous bid.

If Fosborg's firm was holding a position in one or more of those stocks, Sam's big-hearted bid might have helped them maintain support for the stock. There's nothing illegal in what Fosborg did. To do his job properly, though, he should have inquired about the current price of the stock before he passed on Sam's order. Sam, of course, should not have let him place the order without doing so.

These are small mistakes in themselves, and common ones. In our narrative these errors are committed by a novice who is just getting into the market and perhaps should have to pay for learning the hard way. In fact, though, some of the mistakes are committed each day by thousands of investors who should know better.

There are millions of men and women who have prospered substantially by investing in the stock market, quite apart from those "insiders" you read about who have accumulated vast fortunes in Wall Street. Many of the beneficiaries have been "little fellows" much smaller, when they started out, than Sam Webster. They were poorer perhaps, but usually they were wiser.

At the same time there are millions of investors who find that their forays into the stock market are barely fruitful, hardly worth the effort. And there are millions more, of course, who actually lose money. Some lose quite heavily.

The stock market is not a gamble unless you make it so. Owning a portion—a share—of a business involves less risk than owning your own business. The one difference is that you own control of your own business and your success or failure depends on your own talents. In owning stock in someone else's business, you're depending on that other person to manage it well and profitably. This may be all to the good, for most corporations have expert managers.

How about those successful investors—those smug ones?

They have learned all of the caveats. They have built-in-lists of instructions, each beginning with "Thou shalt not . . ." They not only know *how* to buy common stocks; they also know how *not* to buy common stocks.

They have learned that in the stock market there are more things that *you should not do* than there are things that you *should do.*

This can be true of almost anything, of course, but in Wall Street the caveats are more subtle, less obvious. It doesn't take a genius to know that "Thou shalt not" turns off the engines of an airplane when it is in flight. It takes a bit more practical knowledge to know when to turn off the desire for a specific stock when you learn certain things about it.

The cardinal sin for any investor is to enter the marketplace uninformed. Yet that's exactly what bumbling Sam Webster did. Strangely enough, there have been people investing in stocks for years—millions of them—who plunge into investments with no more basic knowledge of what they're doing than Sam had.

The same careful shoppers who spend hours pinching vegetables or fruit, to be certain they are buying their produce wisely, cavalierly spend thousands of dollars buying stocks in companies of which they have at best, only skimpy knowledge. Their sin is compounded when you consider that all the information they need to make sound judgments is readily available and can be garnered with small effort.

Many have been spared knowledge of their inadequacies by a rising market.

The fact that you may have made money on an investment does not necessarily mean that you are a wise investor. Many factors, including sheer luck, may have played a role.

The proper test is whether you can do it again . . . and again . . . and again.

Only in the long haul can you come to know whether you're a wide-awake, wise, sound investor.

Many people are making less money than they could if they would learn to identify their mistakes and correct them.

As for Sam Webster, the newcomer to the market, he should

have written to the New York Stock Exchange and asked for its information booklet on how the market operates and how brokerage firms operate.

It would have been worthwhile, if he lived anywhere in the East, to make a trip to the Exchange to see the many visual aids that are there for his edification, and to join in one of the guided tours that takes guests to the Visitors' Gallery overlooking the trading floor.

He should have asked for the Exchange's list of companies that have paid dividends over a long period of time.

He should have written to a dozen brokerage firms—selected at random from the Yellow Pages, if need be—and asked to be put on their mailing lists for recommended stocks.

He should have informed himself on how to read and interpret the financial news in such excellent sources as the *Wall Street Journal* and the *New York Times,* and how to cull financial tips from *Time* and *Newsweek,* both of which have business sections that are on top of the market, and how to get choice benefits from such technical publications as the excellent weekly, *Barron's,* and the regal *Wall Street Transcript.*

Then and only then should he have sought out a good broker. By that time, from reading those publications, he would have a good idea as to which firm would get his business.

Even then, he should have written to a half-dozen good houses and asked them what they thought they could do for him and his little nest-egg.

Only after careful evaluation of the responses, should he have made his choice.

Too many people enter the stock market without even knowing why or how it functions.

Why is there a stock market? It's not there merely to provide exciting and sometimes profitable action for folks with a few bucks to hazard on the Big Game in Wall Street.

And if General Electric is worth a certain number of hundreds of millions of dollars on Tuesday, making each share worth so much in the marketplace, why should the price rise or fall on Wednesday?

And why should stock prices rise or fall on good or bad news?

Until you have the answers to these questions, it doesn't make sense.

And until it makes sense, you shouldn't try to invest.

III *Picking the Wrong Time to Invest*

The time to develop an affectionate longing for a security is when other people are avoiding it.

Usually, the *wrong* time to decide you want a particular stock is when it has turned popular and when many others share your desire to own it.

This one area—this "going along with the crowd"—causes more problems and heartaches for investors than, possibly, any other factor in trading in the stock market. There's a simple rule: *A popular stock is rarely the best stock to own.* It's easy to chose a wrong stock; it's easier to select the wrong time to buy it.

Speculators can make money by anticipating what the crowd will do. As *inners and outers,* buying stocks in large quantities, they can benefit greatly by anticipating a surge in popularity of a stock and buying either before the crowd gets in or early in the price run-up, and then selling out before the majority realizes that the free ride is over.

This is done all the time, but it is a device to be used only by highly skilled professional Wall Streeters who know the *right* time to make each important move—the right time to buy—and the right time to sell.

Most amateurs who take a fling at this tempting trick, thinking they will profit because they possess inside information on a particular stock, overlook the important fact that you've got to be rich to start with—that only very big purchases pay off for the speculator.

If a stock that is selling for fifty dollars a share suddenly attracts attention, and you, for some reason or other, know in advance that it is going to do so, it's natural to decide to buy a hundred shares and see what happens. If you can keep an open mind about it all, it might be fun to do—and even a little bit profitable.

The trouble is, not many amateurs make such purchases knowing how little they can expect to make on such a deal. The fifty dollar stock will cost you five thousand dollars for one hundred shares, plus commissions. Down in Wall Street, old Pete Professional hears the same report that you did, but he puts up fifty thousand dollars and buys a thousand shares—or maybe it's a hundred thousand dollars for two thousand shares.

You've made your purchase, and you sit and wait. Pete Professional is ready to make his at just the right moment. Then, finally, the anticipated limelight reaches your stock and the crowd notices it and begins to buy. Pete beat them to it by a hair, and his purchase nudged the price up just a bit.

It posts a two point gain!

With your hundred shares, which cost you five thousand dollars, you've made a two hundred dollar profit.

With his thousand shares, Pete Professional has made two thousand dollars—and if he bought two thousand shares, he has made a four thousand dollar profit.

Pete is already thinking about getting out. Looking at your paltry two hundred dollar gain, what are you thinking?

Chances are, you decide to wait some more.

Quite simply, for Pete Professional, it's worthwhile. For the small man, it isn't. Moreover, the man of modest means who has a small amount of money riding on a speculative binge is prone to wait too long. He'll reach for every point of gain, and then sell when it begins to turn down, usually taking more of a loss on the downside than he expected.

The reason for this is that if Pete Professional, with his expert view and access to a continuous flow of information, calculates that the enhanced popularity of the stock will give it a temporary five-point rise, he coldly figures on picking up a three or four point gain and then selling. He can realize a handsome profit by tying up his money for only a few days, as he is trading in large blocks of stock and his profits are ratioed accordingly.

The small fellow rarely has the necessary expertise or the information, to figure out in advance how much he can expect in the way of a gain on a speculative stock, so he plays it by ear and sells on "hunch." Unless, of course, the price turns down suddenly—as ultimately it will—in which case he sells in desperation.

It is doubtful that you, with your five thousand dollar investment, will be content to sell after a three point rise, realizing a profit of only three hundred dollars, minus brokerage commissions. Instead, you'll be more likely to wait and see how high the price will go. By the time you find out, it might be too late.

A point or two before the price of the stock begins to turn down, Pete Professional will have sold out, along with several other professionals like him, pulling support from the stock. When there are big sales like that, the descent in the price of the stock can be much more precipitous than the run-up had been.

Popularity of speculative issues, and even of sturdy blue chips, is usually a temporary and mercurial condition. A stock can turn from a beauty queen to a hag in a matter of minutes, and for no apparent reason. The experts know this, and by careful calculations, they play it safe.

They're in, then they're out, while the average fellow is still reading the quotations in a vain search for a miracle. Miracles do happen in Wall Street. They occur quite frequently, in fact (Xerox, IBM, Hunt Foods, for example.) But the wise investor, particularly the man of modest means, doesn't *gamble* on the fact that some miracle might happen.

But let's back up for a minute. What you're really seeking in the stock market is a long-range investment, one that will pay you regular dividends and at the same time increase in value as the months and years pass. All things considered, that's much preferable to a quick free ride, a fast in-and-out deal. For even when you're successful in the fast-buck enterprise, you're faced with commissions and taxes, and you're still left with cash in hand that needs to be invested. *It is preposterously improvident to simply wait around with cash, looking for some speculative deal.*

Let's assume that you have settled on a stock that you want to buy. You have selected it through the careful processes that are delineated in other chapters of this book. You are confident that this is the stock you really want.

The question remaining is: When is the right time to buy it?

In order to make a proper judgment on the right time, you must first arm yourself with nine figures, three of which you can get from your daily newspaper's table of quotations. The remaining six can be supplied by your broker, or can be gleaned from Standard & Poor's yearbook.

From your newspaper you need the current price of your stock, this year's high and this year's low. From your broker or Standard & Poor's, you'll need the highs and lows of the stock for the last three years. These should be committed to a small table so that you can make proper comparisons.

Let's suppose that ABC Corporation, in which you are interested in investing, produces figures that look like these:

ABC Corporation

		Current Price	18½		
1971 High	23	1971 Low	11
1970 High	27	1970 Low	13
1969 High	19¼	1969 Low	11¾
1968 High	16⅛	1968 Low	8¾

So far it appears that ABC Corporation is a good buy at this time—all other requirements for the stock's purchase having been met. It is four and one-half points below the year's high and eight and one-half points below its high for the last three years. It is seven and one-half points above the year's low.

You would be buying in a *range* that could easily tolerate

improvement in the price of the stock. You would not be buying at the top, nor would you be coming in at the bottom of a stock that might be *sick* for reasons that you have been unable to uncover or perceive.

So far, so good.

Now is the time to turn back to the newspaper lists for the last week or two and check the volume in ABC Corporation stock on a day-to-day basis.

If it appears that the volume was normal—that is, not too high —you can assume that there has been no great flurry of buying to push the price of your stock artificially or temporarily higher than it should be at this time.

Under these conditions, it seems safe to place your order at 18½.

Chances are excellent that you will have picked the right time to buy the stock of ABC Corporation.

You will not have done what most people do—that is, select a stock, check it out and find that it provides a good potential for investment, and then simply place an order to buy it.

This check on the right time to invest is, of course, the last thing that you do before actually buying the stock of your choice, and it may seem that such instructions appear in the wrong part of this narrative. There's a reason for it, for in these days, the timing of purchases is something you have to consider from the first moment you begin your investigation of a stock.

During these times, and probably for many years to come, inflation will be a dominant force in the nation's economy and will reflect its influence on the stock market and on the prices of the stocks that are traded there.

Common stocks provide the perfect hedge against inflation, if purchased at the right time. *They usually inflate in price at the same rate or faster than the economy does.*

To see this in clearer perspective, it is necessary to realize that when there is inflation, the value of money is cheapened, and the value of goods is increased; conversely, when there is depression, the value of goods is cheapened, and the value of money is increased.

In times of inflation, when money is cheapened in value and goods and services become dearer or more costly, the extent of the erosion in the worth of the dollar can be measured by the Cost-of-Living Index prepared by the Bureau of Labor Statistics of the Department of Commerce. If this shows that the cost of living has increased by, say, ten percent over a certain period of time, it means that it requires $1.10 to buy what $1.00 would have bought at the beginning of that period.

It means that your savings, being money, are worth ten percent less than they were at the beginning of that period of time, aside from any interest that was paid on them.

But it also means that, basically, any real estate that you have owned increased in value by ten percent during that same period of time. This holds true of most tangibles, except currency.

Because a common stock represents a share in the ownership of many tangibles, such as plant, equipment, raw materials and finished inventory, it acquires added value for inflation, just the same as real estate does. It usually increases in value as the Cost-of-Living Index climbs.

But because common stock is in itself an almost tangible commodity, and is actively traded in an auction market where it can attract bidders, it acquires an added value in responding to the inflationary upward thrust. *Thus, it traditionally increases at a faster and a higher rate than the actual increase in the cost of living.*

For this reason, and at certain times, the basic measurements for *timing* in the purchase of stock may be changed.

Let's say you're also interested in XYZ Corporation. There are valid reasons. It pays good dividends, and has for years. It is very well managed. It manufactures good products that sell well year after year. It services them adequately. Moreover, it has been working on a revolutionary new product that experts think will be much in demand when it is finished, and you think it's almost time for it to be introduced. There have been a few news stories hinting as much.

You look up the figures and study them in the same manner that you did for ABC Corporation. Here's how they come out on your scratch pad:

	XYZ Corporation		
	Current Price	34½	
1971 High	34½	1971 Low	18
1970 High	24	1970 Low	14
1969 High	29	1969 Low	12
1968 High	23	1968 Low	12

You'll be buying at the high! Moreover, the stock has moved up a whopping sixteen points from its low. Danger signals should flash in your brain!

On the surface it appears that this is no time to buy XYZ Corporation. Perhaps it would be more prudent to back away and wait until it drops a few points.

Inflation may have been playing a role here. You check on that by checking the volume in exactly the same way that you did on ABC Corporation's stock. And you find it has been holding fairly stable during the last couple of weeks.

This, then, is not a case where you will be "following the crowd." The crowd hasn't been after XYZ Corporation—some knowledgable investors, perhaps, armed with the same information that you have, and some portfolio managers, probably, who keep their fingers in these and all similar pies, but obviously the broad public hasn't been attracted to XYZ Corporation—yet.

Under those specific conditions, and again, providing that XYZ Corporation measured up to all other requirements, it would seem that the timing was right to acquire the stock.

The point to remember on both purchases is that you are not a speculator. You are not buying with the intention of selling for a profit in the very near future. While you should always keep an open

mind about switching stocks in your portfolio, and remember that
no one ever went broke taking a profit, your attitude should be that
you are perfectly willing to hold onto a stock for a long period of time
—years, if necessary—in the expectation that there will be a solid,
steady and healthy appreciation in its value, and that its dividends
will be paid.

Fluctuations in price, once you've become the owner of stock,
shouldn't bother you. Fluctuations are for *buying*, not for selling. If
there's a desirable stock whose price is fluctuating, place your order
to buy at two or three points below the market and see if you can
catch it at a bargain. Frequently it's a device that pays off.

A common mistake made even by professionals is to assume
that the prices of securities traded in the stock market and listed by
the Stock Exchange, are either fair or durable. Quite commonly,
they are neither.

Many prices are depressed "bargains" simply because of some
current popular sentiment. Many stocks at any given time are selling
too high for exactly the same reason. These conditions will change
from time to time and a stock that is favored today may well be
widely regarded as a "dog" six months from now.

The Stock Exchange is an auction market, and at any auction,
prices are supposed to fluctuate. Unless there's some special support
for a stock or, as rarely happens these days, some manipulating is
going on behind scenes, the price of a security will be governed
mostly by what the biggest buyers at the auction are thinking. These
are the investment dealers, trust managers, portfolio managers for
pension funds, mutual funds, investment trusts. There's tugging and
hauling that goes on among these experts as they try to gauge the
market, and because of this, there will be moderate rises and dips
in prices for even the most stable and sturdy securities.

The stock market is also subjected to fads, almost as readily as
the fashion market.

Faddism in the market produces quick profits for some and
sudden losses for others. When the flurry of tickertape has settled,
it is usually found that the winners in the fad game are the old-line

professionals who knew what they were doing, and the losers are smart-apple amateurs who thought, mistakenly, that they could beat the market the fast way.

There's no fast way for most. There is an easy way, as we shall see, but it requires patience and time.

IV *Picking the Wrong Company*

There are about 1,300 corporate stocks listed on the New York Stock Exchange and approximately one thousand on the American Stock Exchange, providing the potential investor with a mind-boggling smorgasbord of securities. In addition there are countless thousands of other stocks traded in New York's Over-the-Counter market and on regional stock exchanges across the land.

What motivates the ordinary investor to buy a specific security is a question that has always fascinated Wall Streeters, and has, in fact, occupied the studies of this author for nearly a quarter-century.

No real research has ever been done on the subject, though motivation is, by all odds, the biggest factor (outside of the possession of money) governing the buying and selling of all securities. The big, rich brokerage and investment industry operates more or less in the dark, handling the trades of millions of customers whose motivations are relatively unknown.

Detailed market studies have been made so that when a housewife buys a can of tuna fish, the marketers know exactly what made her do it. This is not so in the securities industry. There, it is simply assumed that a purchaser or seller of stocks knows what he is about and initiates his action to buy or sell solely for making profit or taking a deliberate tax loss.

While the profit motive is transcending, of course, there must be other reasons why, at the same time that one investor is calling his broker to order a hundred shares of Radio Corporation of America, another is calling a different broker to order a hundred shares of Goodrich Tire and Rubber Company. What motivated one to buy RCA? What motivated the other to buy Goodrich?

It is *assumed* by the brethren in the brokerage community that these purchasers know exactly what they are doing and are buying for specific reasons based on well-formed judgments, whether those judgments be good or bad, right or wrong.

This may be far from the truth. With no reflection intended on either corporation, the two individuals may be making extremely unwise purchases for that time, and in relation to their own holdings.

On four separate occasions, spaced in a period of more than a decade, this writer conducted small straw polls among investors to inquire into their motives for buying specific stocks. The inquiries were for the purpose of preparing, one day, a revealing feature for the *New York Herald Tribune,* where the author served as Business and Financial Editor. Since that newspaper no longer exists, the results of the poll have never before been published.

In no way should this be regarded as either a scientific or a meaningful study, as the samples were taken at random and at widely-spaced periods of time, with total disregard to the backgrounds of those polled, their sophistication or their income classifications.

Experience dictates that one may assume that an investor of considerable means has access to more valuable information about a company's stock, if only because he can afford better research. If he's a big trader, his broker is likely to dig a little deeper in his behalf to find the facts. Just as the best customer in a restaurant merits the friendliest smile from the headwaiter and gets the best corner table, the biggest customers in Wall Street receive the broker's most serious consideration and the largest share of his time and effort.

If my polls had any degree of accuracy whatsoever, it appears that only about ten percent of those who invest do so on the basis of careful and thorough research, including consideration of and elimination of other potential purchases at the same time.

These were individuals who had money to invest and who shopped around carefully and made what they considered to be wise selections.

In the first survey, exactly ten percent—eight out of eighty people—said they bought stocks only after thorough research that included more than "surface" investigation and examination. In the second survey the figure fell to eight percent of the sample. It was eleven percent in both the third and fourth surveys.

Lumping the remainder into one whole unit—those who did not buy stock as the result of extensive research—and averaging the results of four surveys, this is how the decisions to buy stocks were reached:

Reasons For Buying Stock:	Percentage
-Bought on advice of broker	31%
-Bought on advice of trusted friend	27
-Bought because liked products of company	10
-Bought because had read some good reports about the company	8
-Bought because liked the company's advertising campaigns	7
-Bought because liked prospects for the industry in which company operates	7
-Bought because wanted representative company of that industry in his portfolio	6
-Bought as a result of following a hunch and doing some (a little) research	2
-Merely played a hunch	2
	100

If the four separate polls have any shred of validity (and at the very least they reflect an honest cross-section) it means that ninety percent of the people who bought stock during a certain period and who were queried by the author based their purchases on what must be considered to be capricious reasons. Whether they are a true representation of all who purchased stock on those days—that is, that ninety percent of *all* purchasers were capricious—remains a question requiring more expert evaluation than the author can provide.

The thirty-one percent who bought stocks on the advice of a broker at least spent their money with professional guidance, which is more than any of the others can claim to have done.

Whether a broker's recommendation is of any value depends in great measure on how important you are to him as a customer.

Quite commonly, a *broker's recommendation* means merely that the broker has researched and analyzed a stock and on the basis of several standard measurements, has found it satisfactory as an investment.

It is not unusual for a broker to recommend stock in which he has taken a position himself. This need not mean that the stock is not a good one to buy for investment purposes. Quite the contrary, it can, under certain circumstances, indicate that it is a desirable purchase. Brokers who make bad guesses about stocks don't last long. But buying a stock because someone else likes it is not the wisest policy to follow in the stock market.

"Ask The Man Who Owns One," may have been a great slogan for selling Packard Motor Cars, but it has no place in Wall Street. You usually fare better by buying a stock that only a relatively few people find attractive at the time of your purchase, in the hope that more will "discover" it after your purchase has been confirmed.

There are popular examples that can be cited.

Showman Billy Rose became a multi-millionaire with his huge accumulation of the common stock of American Telephone & Telegraph Company only because he bought it when it was popularly thought of in Wall Street as that "dull, grey old lady, Ma Bell." Ma Bell had been slumbering in her rocking chair for years, paying out a predictable nine dollar annual dividend, about as inspiring as a fat, lazy altered tomcat on a warm hearth.

When old Ma Bell stripped off her concealing Mother Hubbard and emerged as a spectacularly luscious queen, filled with exciting new ideas (in the laboratory, men) there was a great rush to buy AT&T stock. It was too late for the *real* goodies in Ma Bell by the time the brokers got around to recommending it. Billy Rose, and a few like him, had discerned the great beauty hiding beneath the drab garment of the dull, grey old lady of Wall Street. Such discernment comes from research.

Those who bought stock on the advice of a trusted friend were almost as numerous as those who bought it on the advice of a trusted broker. Needless to say, the degree of capriciousness is enhanced considerably, for one assumes that brokers know *something* about the investment profession, while a friend may have no skill in the market whatsoever. A good track record is not necessarily proper evidence of skill.

Friends who become excited and pleased when a stock they have bought gains a few points, frequently think they are doing a favor to recommend it. More often than not, it's no favor. In many cases the bloom is off the rose by the time the second friend comes along and buys the stock, and he gets it at its peak price.

Another thing to remember about the advice of a friend: "Misery loves company." Many people believe that if they can induce a wide enough circle of friends to buy the stock they hold it will escalate in price. Suffice it to say that while this is true in theory, it would require many more friends than even the friendliest of men can hope to have to seriously affect the price of a stock traded on a major exchange.

The ten percent who bought stock in a corporation because they liked its products were at least thinking constructively, though it is a limited measurement (many good companies don't make consumer products), and it is dangerous to make a subjective judgment about products. Only sales records provide proper evaluation, for what appeals to you may not appeal to the vast majority of consumers.

Put the thought aside for future reference, however, for it will come up again in these discussions. The company that has a successful record of introducing new, good and popular products is, in the long run, what you're looking for. It is one of the measurements, and an important one, you will apply against a stock when you are a sophisticated investor.

The eight percent who bought stock because they read some good reports about the company fell for a public relations pitch, and in so doing, they reveal that they do not fully understand the functions and operations of the modern corporation where public relations is an essential part of existence.

Good reports about listed corporations circulate constantly and are printed in good faith and as a matter of information in the most respected media. These reports emanate from the public relations departments of the big corporations and from Madison Avenue and Wall Street public relations firms. There are nearly as many public relations houses in Wall Street specializing exclusively in corporate and financial "news" as there are on Madison Avenue.

While there are legal restrictions on what—and how much— may be writen about a company, particularly when it is involved in various phases of its financing, the idea is to maintain a steady flow of press copy to help sustain a corporation's good image. It is an essential part of management's job.

A good share of the company's net worth is in the fair market value of its treasury stock. The price of its stock in the marketplace determines how much money and at what cost it can borrow for operating and expanding. In addition, the personal wealth of the members of top management of a corporation is tied up in stock and stock options so that not only their careers but their fortunes depend on keeping the market attractive for their stock. This is accomplished through "good reports."

A negative judgment can be made about such public relations fare, however. When sales and profits fall off, corporations generally tighten their belts by cutting back on public relations and advertising budgets. A company that cuts back too severely on its public relations expenditures may be considered by the average investor to be a poorer-than-usual investment prospect.

On the face of such evidence, it would seem that such a company is poorly managed. There might be other reasons for the cutback, of course, and this is something you'd have to dig into. But if you notice that a certain company has ceased to gain any attention in the news columns of the financial sections of your newspapers, or if you read in the advertising news column that a company has cut back on its advertising and promotional budget, then by all means harbor the suspicion that it isn't being managed well.

Those who bought stock because they liked a company's advertising forgot about the Edsel. Period. Or Kaiser. Double Period.

Some of the poorest and most irritating advertising sells the most products. Some of the finest, most pleasing, seemingly most-persuasive ads fail to do a thing for sales. Year after year the Colgate Palmolive Company is right up among the leaders in sales in the soap industry; year after year Colgate Palmolive pays for some of the most irritating and immature television commercials to go out over the air.

Not many years ago Sinclair Oil Company ran a costly nation-wide advertising campaign describing the great national parks and urging motorists to drive to them—after filling up with Sinclair gasoline, of course. The ads were so attractive that Sinclair was nearly overwhelmed with requests for reprints of them. This turned into a costly added operation for the company.

When all the facts and figures were tallied and an assessment was made, Sinclair officials learned that while the ads were an outstanding success, the campaign was accompanied by a steady decline in the sales of Sinclair gasoline and its automotive petroleum products line.

The seven percent who bought their stock because they liked the prospects for the industry in which the corporation operates were on the right track—but it was a siding they mistakenly thought was the main line.

To pick an industry that holds promising potential is a good start. To pick out one company in that industry without thoroughly investigating it and measuring it against other companies in the same industry, is like buying a ten year old car without test-driving it.

The same may be said of the six percent who bought a company's stock because they wanted a representative of that industry in their portfolio. Suppose the company is burdened with debt? Suppose it has a record for poor research and development? Suppose it is poorly managed? Selecting the right industry is important, but not nearly so important as picking the right company in the right industry.

The author was impressed, during the course of his sampling, when a total of four percent said they bought their stock on a hunch.

These people are gamblers, and they admit it. They must pick their horses at the race track in much the same fashion, depending on Lady Luck to bring in a winner now and then.

There *are* gamblers in the stock market, of course. Some of them make out all right. Most don't. Generally you don't hear much about them because being unsuccessful in Wall Street is not as bad as being unsuccessful at the race track. At the track, when you lose, you don't get any part of your money back. In Wall Street, though you may sell at a loss, and you get something back on the sale. You never run out of the money; you're more or less assured of at least having "Show money."

The most important thing, though, is that while chance plays a major role at the race track, there need be little risk-taking in Wall Street.

If you know how to sniff out a good stock, stalk it, research it, analyze it, and buy it at the right time, there's small chance that you will lose money, and good chance that you'll make money.

It's nearly as simple as that.

V Don't Become
an "Insider"

One of the most popular misconceptions about Wall Street is
the belief that *insiders* have access to more vital information—that
is, *the* vital information of what and when to buy, and when to sell
—than do ordinary traders more distantly removed from the scene
of the action.

Don't you believe it.

Few of the real insiders have become rich because of what they
have learned on the inside. *Some* have, of course, but their numbers
are not large. In days gone by, many were able to take advantage of
what the professionals call a "free ride," but in recent years the
Securities and Exchange Commission has kept an eagle eye on the
situations that normally would offer such special advantages to the
select, and *free riding* being illegal these days, the agency clamps
down hard on any who try it.

The favorite free ride in earlier days was taken on new issues.
When an underwriter brought out a new issue of stock in a company
that had, by performance or some other act, attracted the attention
of the investing public, there was predictably a pent-up demand for
the stock that caused it to be oversubscribed. It was virtually a
foregone conclusion that upon "going public," the value of its stock
would rise as the price was bid up.

Let's say the company was issuing a million shares of stock at
ten dollars a share, and the underwriters sold the shares at discount
to brokers throughout the Street. The brokers in turn offered the
shares to the public at the ten dollar price.

Then let's further assume that two days before the stock was scheduled to go public, the brokers counted up and found they had received orders for a million and a half shares, a half million more than were available.

To protect all customers, the brokers would ration the stock, placing limits on the amount that each customer could buy.

Any observer with half an eye would be able to predict that on the day of the public offering the price would rise, perhaps by as much as ten points or more.

Insiders would wait until the day before the public offering, then place orders for as many shares as the traffic would allow, but would simultaneously place a sell order for fifteen or twenty dollars, meaning that when the price of the stock reached that specific figure, their shares would be sold automatically.

Since this price would be reached the very day of the public offering of the stock, the trade would have gone through without any cash changing hands. The buyer of a thousand shares of stock would own fifteen thousand dollars, if he sold out at fifteen dollars, and he would owe his broker ten thousand dollars. He would have a profit of five thousand dollars without having put up a dime. Thus came the term, *free ride.*

Today the SEC requires that you pay for stock within forty-eight hours. After the sale of stock it's unlikely that you'll get your check for a week or more, so you really do have to pay for the stock that you buy. Also, when there is an oversubscription, the SEC examiners scrutinize the lists of buyers and if they spot the name of someone who was connected with the underwriters or one of the primary brokers, they inquire to find out if he was acting on inside information.

Yet there is nothing illegal about buying a stock and placing a specific *sell order* on it. Thousands of people have to be aware of what is going on when a new issue is over-subscribed—brokers, their salesmen, customers' men, analysts, researchers, and armies of secretaries as well as messengers. Any one of them may anticipate the oversubscription and seek to make an easy and quick profit on the deal.

The records do not show that many of them ever got rich acting on this "insider's information," at least not since the requirement that the stock be paid for within two days. It takes too much hard cash to purchase a sufficient amount of new-issue stock to make it worthwhile.

Another kind of insider has come into existence with the growth of the huge institutional investors, the mutual funds and trust funds. When an investment manager who handles a multi-million dollar portfolio decides he wants to buy a specific stock in quantity, it is quite likely that the price of that stock will move up on his persistent bidding. Of course, the manager won't go into the market and place an enormous order—this would propel the stock's price through the roof. Instead he will buy varying amounts of the stock over a period of time, keeping a careful eye on the market as he does so.

He will have to plan his strategy, however. He will confer with his researcher, with his market analyst, with his investment counselors, and others. His secretaries will take copious memoranda and write numerous letters. By the time he is ready to move, a great many insiders are aware of what he is planning to do.

It is possible for them to buy that specific stock and hold it during the period that the portfolio manager is acquiring it, expecting it to appreciate a few points.

Such an investor has a strong enemy in the manager of the account who will do everything in his power to keep the price of the stock level—or even lower, if possible—during the period he has planned for purchasing it. It becomes a case of amateurs pitting their wits against a wily professional, and usually the professional wins. The stock doesn't gain much.

However, the real investor (a non-speculator) might do well, under such circumstances, to hold onto his stock for the long haul, because if the institutional professional believes it is worthy of investment, it means he is expecting a good, solid increase in the stock's value in the future.

Sadly, it is not the nature of the person who buys on insiders' tips to be a genuine investor. He is a speculator, pure and simple, and in the case described above, he most likely would sell without a profit—or with only a small gain—as soon as the portfolio-buying was completed.

The Securities and Exchange Commission is militant about insider information that is not available to others that might affect the value of a specific stock, either up or down. It insists that when corporations deal with the public, they make *full disclosure,* and this is interpreted to mean *anything* and *everything* that may have a bearing on the company, its buildings, its equipment, its holdings, its officers, its products, its practices and policies, and its stock.

If it does not wish to face the prospect of having trading in its stock suspended, and fines and even jail sentences for its officials, a company dare not make disclosure of vital information about itself to *some* persons without making it simultaneously available to *all* people.

There is no reason, therefore, to believe that in the general operations of Wall Street you can benefit more by being an insider than you can by keeping your eyes open and reading the daily file of news in the *Wall Street Journal* and the financial news in your local daily newspaper.

Indeed, there is reason to suspect that a well-trained and knowledgable investor, if he could be supplied with the daily media and had ready access to communications, would fare better from an isolated tropical island where, undistracted, he would see his investments in their proper perspective.

So tough is the Securities and Exchange Commission in insisting on full disclosure to all parties at the same time that it brought a celebrated case in 1969 and 1970 against a prominent Wall Street brokerage firm and a leading American aircraft manufacturer because of a news "leak" by the broker.

It was not a leak of information in the sense that the public has come to understand it in relation to the press. The broker, one of the Street's most reputable firms, had sent its aircraft corporation researcher for a routine visit to the plants and an interview with company officials.

While there, the researcher learned that sales and earnings were slipping and that the manufacturer would likely report lower earnings in the next quarterly report.

This is valid information, certainly, and important to investors. It was gained by digging out facts and asking the right questions of the right people.

Dutifully the researcher reported his findings to his superiors.

Just as dutifully his superiors committed this information to a newsletter and sent it out to their favored customers.

Next day there was notable "dumping" of the stock as the people who were informed of what would be in the quarterly report took their profits and sold out.

After investigation, the SEC brought charges against both the broker and the corporation for violation of the regulation that requires full disclosure to all parties simultaneously.

The broker contended that if the researcher, through his own enterprise, dug up facts that had value, the broker, who is in the business of transmitting such important facts to legitimate customers, had a right to use those facts as he saw fit.

No, said the SEC; in effect a fact is a fact, and in the investment business, it belongs to everyone. The researcher might have used the facts for his own *personal* advantage, but he could not make them known to *some* without making them known to all.

The one area where it might pay to be an insider and where you could profit by selling stock if you owned it, is in having access to the so-called secret *No-Action Letters* issued by the Securities and Exchange Commission.

These usually involve the intended sale of unregistered stock by an official of a corporation, stock that he owns as an organizer or that he acquired through options.

To sell such stock he must first write to the SEC's Division of Corporate Finance and inquire if the agency would take action against him for disposing of a certain number of shares of his stock.

He lists the reasons why he wishes to sell. If these are valid reasons, the SEC informs him that it will take no action—hence the term No-Action Letters.

By regulation these letters are kept secret because more often than not the reason for wanting to sell is highly personal. A man may have large hospital bills, or an alimony settlement, or heavy legal fees for a wayward child, and he does not wish to have such information made either official or public.

It is obvious that anyone who owns stock in this man's corporation is going to get a secret *watering* of his equity. If there are, for instance, ten million registered shares outstanding, and the corporate official adds a million unregistered shares to the total in the open market, the stock is watered by nearly one-tenth.

Anyone who could have access to the No-Action Letter involved in the sale would profit by selling out his shares prior to the watering.

For thirty-seven years the SEC through its No-Action Letters, permitted corporate insiders to sell unregistered shares on the open market in total secrecy. In Fall 1970, however, bowing to considerable legal pressure, the agency decided to make the letters public— but after a lapse of thirty days—too late, in many cases, to do the unaware stockholder any good.

The SEC, like any large government agency, moves slowly to change its policies. This, in the long haul, is probably all to the good.

The day likely will come when the big agency will withhold the *reasons* why a corporate official wishes to sell, but will make known the fact that he does intend to sell a specific number of shares of his unregistered stock.

Until that day, however, the content of a No-Action Letter is valuable information.

In older days when *pools* of stock traders were formed—that is a group of professionals with a lot of money, influence and know-how—one of the most effective manipulative devices was in *selling short*. They would join together to bid the price of a stock up and then sell it short in order to make a profit on the speculation.

People who had inside information as to what the pool operators were doing could, indeed, cash in on the goodies, but they had to move precisely in unison with the pool, or suffer losses.

Usually the pool operators would risk very little of their own money in planning a manipulated short sale. It must be remembered that in the days when several dozen daily newspapers covered Wall Street directly, and financial editors were not the highly trained specialists that they are today, it was much easier to "plant" stories in the press that would affect specific issues of stock.

The pool operators customarily stimulated public interest in a stock by generating carefully planned publicity about it, and then backed it up by creating considerable activity in the market.

This activity would be accomplished with what came to be known as *wash sales*. Now outlawed by the Securities and Exchange Commission, a wash sale consisted simply of buying, then immediately selling, large blocks of a particular stock. This would create the impression of a large volume of activity in the stock, something that inevitably attracts the attention of the unsophisticated public.

As the public bought, the price would rise. The pool operators, their fingers on the market's pulse, would wait until the price of the stock rose about as high as they thought it would climb, and then would begin selling it short, pounding the price down to a point where they could buy it back at a handsome profit.

Not only are wash sales illegal today, but among SEC reforms is one that effectively prevents abuse of the right to sell a stock short. This is a simple regulation that says, in effect, that a stock can be sold short only on a rising market—only on the *uptick*.

Thus, all things considered, it doesn't seem to pay to strive to be an insider these days. Most activities involving the inside operations of Wall Street are conducted in a goldfish bowl before the ever-suspicious eye of the Securities and Exchange Commission. And most insider activities that might once have been profitable are now illegal.

Therefore be suspicious of any "inside tips" that may come your way. You most likely are being baited up for a sucker play.

The theme that will be brought home again and again in this book is—don't be a gambler, be an investor.

To be an investor you don't need any of the so-called inside information.

What you need is facts, specifics, and simple arithmetic.

VI *What . . .*
Use Technical Advice?

The thirty million or more Americans who own common stocks, plus the several million foreigners who have invested in American corporations, have created such an insatiable demand for information about the securities business that a great "informational market" has grown up and enormous numbers of words are committed to paper each year, producing millions of dollars for those who write and disseminate them.

In thus pumping money through the arteries of the nation's economy, they serve their greatest usefulness.

Their value to the average trader is to be seriously questioned.

The intelligence of a small investor who relies on these technical advisories is to be questioned even more seriously, yet apparently millions of them breathlessly await regular "technical market analysis" from the experts.

If you read this technical advice carefully, you're likely to learn that the stock market will go up if it doesn't go down, that is, considering all the factors and based on normal expectations. On the other hand, it might go down if it doesn't go up, in the opinion of some knowledgable chartists (nameless), though unforeseen factors may play a basic role in placating current demand and erasing pressures to sell.

Eh?

How much is that information worth to you?

You can buy it in market letters that range in price from twenty-five dollars a year to twenty-five dollars a week. It is pumped out by scores of service agencies, including the large brokerage houses, but the brokers send it out free of charge to their customers. That's the fairest price charged for most technical market analysis.

Whether the stock market will go up or down next week is of some importance to an investor if he is about to trade—that is, either buy or sell—but it is of only casual interest to him if he has investments in a portfolio that he intends to keep and build on.

About the only people concerned with the week-to-week forecasts of the market are managers of big investment funds, and if they know their business, they are much more knowledgable about what will happen than the experts who grind out the forecasts.

Even the big managers can be misled and tricked by their own research and observation, for the market is not—repeat, is *not*—predictable. Its day-to-day and week-to-week trend is no more reliable than wind direction in New England, where Mark Twain observed that if you don't like the weather, just wait a minute.

That's because the fluctuations in the market are emotional and not pragmatic. They are caused by psychological forces. The responses by traders to outside influences result in "psychosomatic symptoms" on the trading floor.

An unexpected paragraph in a speech by the President, or an important member of the Cabinet or Congress, can send the market soaring or plummeting. The decision of a leading institutional investor to buy or sell can elevate prices or erode them. Bad weather in some parts of the nation that will affect the commodities market can also affect the stock market, or segments of it.

Anyone, therefore, who attempts to predict market activity is engaging in something bordering on madness.

If you trade on a day-to-day basis, you need to have the best available educated guesses on what the market might do. If you are a professional trader, you are obliged to watch the swings closely and do your buying on the downside and your selling on the up.

But this is not for most. The average investor should be more interested in the long-range market trend, rather than the day-to-day or week-to-week movement. Do the experts think that over the long haul the market prices will rise? If so, they're called *bulls* and their view is said to be *bullish*. Or do they think that in the long-range view, prices will be lower? If so, they're known as *bears*, and their attitude is said to be *bearish*. If they think the market is on a plateau and won't change much in the long months ahead, when do they see an end to the plateau, and are they bullish or bearish about the post-plateau future?

You will want to base your own investing policies on the long-haul forecasts. Perhaps you have selected a stock that you want to buy and add to your portfolio for a few years, but its price has been under the influence of a strong bull market for some time. You think it's too high.

You expect that sooner or later you will be able to buy it at a more favorable price. Under such circumstances you'd be interested in knowing what the real experts think is going to be the terminal point of the bull market. Then, with a downtrend, you would also be interested in knowing when it would end, because you should buy stocks at some point between the onset of the bear trend and its terminal point, hoping to get the best possible prices.

But even then it may be useless information, for your stock may not behave the way the market leaders are doing. It may hold its price, or even rise against the market. It may post gains for the simple reason that others have come to the same conclusion about that stock that you have, and have also decided to buy it.

To become too involved with watching the technical side of the market, its ups and downs and sidewise movements, is like over-studying the theory of aerodynamics but never learning to fly a plane.

Fly it—but don't spend too much time learning its engineering principles.

The point is a simple one: *If you're investing properly, if you're picking your stocks because of the soundness of the company, your consideration of the market's ups and downs is only secondary. You buy because of the strength of a company, not because of the strength of the stock market.*

It may be necessary to keep reminding yourself that the stock market is merely an auction place and that you are not "investing in the stock market" as the common expression would have it—you are investing in companies, and in their people, products, real estate, financial records and markets. These things have specific values that do not change on a day-to-day basis just because General Motors gained two points or American Telephone & Telegraph lost five. The functions of the market are for professionals. Professionals are traders. You are an investor.

You do need *some* market advice, of course, and a long-haul technical appraisal from an expert is necessary for your guidance in the most efficient handling of your own portfolio. The one you can get at no charge, the one sent to you periodically by your own broker, will most likely provide all the information you need, although some of the brokers' advisories are meaningless and dreadfully written. If yours is bad, write to another broker and ask to be put on his mailing list. You'll probably get his advisories.

Here's an example of a good one, written by Edwin F. Thrall, Jr., of F. S. Moseley & Company, Boston:

General Market Summary: Since early October when virtually all of the market averages reached their highs for the rally initiated in May, prices have been gradually trending downward. Although subject, of course, to brief spells of strength (particularly around election time) it is the opinion of this writer that the market is now in the process of making a shorter term downward move which will provide a successful test of the May lows and prepare the way for the initiation of a new bull market.

The past several issues of this report have stressed that, although the market appeared to be near the end of this very severe bear phase, it did not seem to have sufficient power to continue into a new long-term uptrend from the upsurge of the past four months. Instead it has seemed technically more probable (by these methods) that the market would need to endure one more phase of weakness before decisively beginning a reliable and long-lasting uptrend.

Thus, within the context of this technical rationale, it appears that the overall market action is now proceeding with the expected shorter

term downtrend toward the vicinity of the previous May lows in order
to generate additional long-term power and to provide also an effective
demonstration that the underlying support necessary to launch a primary uptrend does exist.

In essence, this gives you what you need to know.

If you want to buy some stock, you know that the bear market
will continue and you can get a bargain price for some time to come.

If you want to sell, or if you want to collateralize your stock,
you know that it would be better to wait until after those "May lows"
are reached.

In the second paragraph of Mr. Thrall's technical advisory you
get a pretty good idea of what he thinks about that bear market. He
comes right out with a prediction (a valid one, it turned out). Such
information, to a small investor, is of good value in planning his
moves.

Let me give you an example of a technical appraisal that would
confuse me if I were a small investor seeking information. It was
written by a top technical analyst—a much respected one—employed by a large New York brokerage firm. The report begins:

> *Stock Market*—The market continues to correct and is staying
> pretty much in line with our expectations. Interestingly enough, and
> perhaps a sign of the underlying strength currently being disguised by
> erratic market performance and temporary economic fog, the selling
> pressure has been restricted to a lateral range. Weakness has been more
> a development of declining buying pressure. Market weakness resulting
> from such a combination of flat selling pressure and declining buying
> pressure usually is a characteristic of a bull phase rather than one repre-
> sentative of a bear phase. Viewed from the near-term standpoint, how-
> ever, we continue to look for retracement, spaced by rally periods, as the
> corrective influences remain in force. Conservation of capital is all
> important at this time in order to take advantage of favorable buying
> points in the weeks ahead.

This gentleman is saying, in essence, what Mr. Thrall said, but
like a sports writer, he has fallen into the habit of using inner-circle

jargon that makes his report "smarter" than it is illuminating. On the other hand, his last sentence is a valuable one, or it was at the time it was sent out to his clients.

Hopefully, some profited by it.

Communication is all-important in the investment business, because facts and information are the twin fuels that power the entire apparatus. The science of communication has been perfected in Wall Street, but not the art. Using a language that is capable of being thrillingly precise, many of those who write analytical reports manage, somehow, to bewilder even the most painstaking reader.

One ironic reason for this is that the writers are inhibited by myriad rules, regulations and caveats laid down by the SEC and the New York Stock Exchange in the interest of fairness and accuracy. Perhaps they are over-supervised.

Far more important to you as a small investor are the reports of the securities research departments of brokerage firms, as well as special reports put out by qualified securities analysts.

These deal with specific companies, and they present detailed information on their managements, their financial structures, their product lines, their competitors, their markets. They also usually report on the industry within which the company operates.

They may be the product of one man in a research department, or they may represent a report jointly prepared by several experts. They provide excellent background material for the small investor and apprise him of facts that he might have to spend a great deal of time, effort and money digging out by himself.

These reports are sent out at no charge by brokerage houses to their customers and others who request them. Other reports prepared by professional analysts are offered for sale to the public. By and large, the research analysis that you get from a reputable broker is just as good for your purposes as the kind you pay for through a private research firm.

Picked at random, here is an example of a brokers' report that represents an abundance of valuable information to the average investor. It was written on October 28, 1970, by Harry W.

Laubscher of Walston & Company, Inc., so remember that it is now outdated. It is used here solely to illustrate what a good report can provide for you with relative economy of words, so that you don't have to waste time reading through a lot of detail.

> *Supermarkets*—These 20th Century novelties trace their origins back to the days of the early 1930's when groups of food merchants would band together under one roof to cut down on overhead costs and attract customers seeking a combination of low prices and one-stop food shopping. In the intervening years, the supermarket food chains have expanded at a rapid pace, attempting to keep up with a fast-rising standard of living and a burgeoning population. Expansion was carried to excess and before long there were just too many food stores. Thus, profits sagged, and growth, for the industry as a whole, was less than dramatic—despite the addition of various innovations such as trading stamps and discount operations.
>
> The average consumer spends twenty-one percent of each dollar earned on food and beverages. It is the largest single item in the consumer's budget. This accounts for food stores constituting the largest business in the United States today, with sales of more than eighty-two billion dollars last year. But its profit performance has not been as outstanding. Recently, however, this profit picture has been changing and for the better. Sales for the first half of this year were up almost ten percent over a year ago and earnings, also, are running ahead of 1969 results. In this promising industry two situations merit consideration for investment purchase: *Winn-Dixie Stores* and *Grand Union.*

Note that Mr. Laubscher has given you an excellent capsule not only of the industry itself, but of past and present performance. He has provided facts that you can apply for measurement against about any food store chain you wish to consider. For example, if you have had your eye on a different food chain, you'll want to check whether its sales increased by more than ten percent during the first half of 1970.

His report continues:

> WINN-DIXIE STORES—WIN (34)—Without a doubt, this company has one of the outstanding records in the retailing industry. Located

largely in the southeastern part of the country, the chain now comprises a total of 816 stores and fifty additional units are expected to be opened during the current fiscal year. In addition, remodeling of older units will be accelerated to maintain a proper competitive stance within the industry.

In the fiscal year ended June, 1970, Winn-Dixie had sales of $1.4 billion, up thirteen percent over fiscal 1969 results. Earnings also advanced to a reported $2.18 a share. With profits for the first quarter of the 1971 fiscal year showing a gain of seventeen percent over year-earlier results, the outlook now exceeds previous projections, and earnings for the current fiscal year are estimated to exceed $2.35 a share. This strongly suggests another increase in the $1.68 a share dividend rate may be anticipated some time next year. Backed by a highly competent management team, and located in one of the faster growing sections of the country, the shares of Winn-Dixie Corp. are considered above average in attraction for investment purchase.

Technically, an area of extensive support has been created by congestion in the 34–31 zone. Although there is near-term resistance indicated by overhanging supply at 36–37, there is an investment price objective at 42–44 initially.

GRAND UNION—GUX (25)—Already the tenth largest retailer in the United States, Grand Union is accelerating its growth. The chain has 532 outlets, all of which are located in 11 eastern states, Washington, D.C. and Puerto Rico. In addition, Grand Union operated 31 discount stores under the Grand Way name. Other operations include Triple-S Stamps, 32 Patio restaurants and a twenty-nine percent interest in Eastern Shopping Centers, Inc. For the fiscal year ending February, 1971, earnings are expected to reach a new peak near $2.50 a share up from $2.30 last year. An additional increase in the eighty-cent annual dividend is anticipated, not only in view of the continued improvement in profits, but also in reflection of the fact that dividends have been increased in each of the last eighteen years.

From a technical standpoint, GUX has considerable overhead supply which could make the advance somewhat tedious. However, stocks more often than not rise into supply and we are applying an investment price objective of 32–34. There is good support against downside pressures in the 22–20 range.

The "WIN" that appears at the beginning of the first paragraph on Winn-Dixie is the stock ticker symbol for Winn-Dixie and the

(34) is the price of the stock at the time the report was prepared.

Anyone who had been thinking about adding some food or retailing stocks to his portfolio would have found valuable information in Mr. Laubscher's report.

However, this report—or any good report—provides insufficient information on which to solely base an investment judgment. There are many unanswered questions about Winn-Dixie and Grand Union that should be resolved before making a decision. These things you will learn as we progress in the book.

Unfortunately, a great many people buy stock with much less information than is presented in the average researcher's report— and not all are as well-documented as Mr. Laubscher's. Far too many people buy stock armed only with the facts they have picked up from friends, or tidbits of information they have gleaned from the welter of reports.

Buying a medical book won't make you a doctor. So don't regard yourself as a Wall Street expert just because you read some expert's report.

VII *Loading Up at the Smorgasbord*

When, as a buyer, you first approach the stock market with its massive list of corporations, you will be bewildered by the magnitude of the selection offered to you. You can buy any one of more than 1,300 common stocks listed on the New York Stock Exchange or more than one thousand on the American Stock Exchange.

How do you make a choice from this potpourri of offerings?

The average person doesn't save his money for the purpose of buying a specific stock. He squirrels money away as best he can until he has accumulated enough to invest. Sometimes he gets an assist, as Sam and Adele Webster did from the legacy from Sam's Aunt Martha.

Then, suddenly, one day there seems to be enough money available. It makes sense for you to invest some of it. You have learned a little about the market and you know you shouldn't rely exclusively on your broker. You should be able to talk to him in his own language, and though you may be guided by his suggestions, you want to make the ultimate decision yourself.

Do you want to buy oils? Food chains? Electronics companies? Appliance manufacturers? Hardware makers? Automotive companies? Textiles? Utilities? Rails? Financial companies? You name it, and they've got it. They've not only got it, they've got much more than you can possibly cope with.

There's a smorgasbord of offerings, and you have only one small plate. What are you going to put on it?

At this moment will come the realization that even if you've managed to pick up some working knowledge of the functions of the stock market, you know very little about the operations of individual American corporations.

Some of the most familiar names suddenly belong to strangers. Good old AT&T—what do you *really* know about it? Standard Oil of New Jersey, now there's virtually a household name, having something to do with the Rockefeller family. But what do you know about SONJ? Who is the president now? What kind of management team does it have? Is it making money out of its vast holdings and its complex distribution network? How does it shape up against its competitors?

It's your money that you're putting on the line, now.

If you dig a little under the surface you find that some of the companies you liked aren't listed companies any longer because they're now part of a conglomerate corporation. And then when you check the conglomerates you discover they're not doing what you had supposed. Some book publishing companies are in the oil business. Railroads are in the canning business. Canners are in oil and timber.

It's no longer a matter of merely liking a product or a company or even an industry, for some of the big conglomerates straddle many industries.

Later on you will learn what to look for in a particular company. At this point all you want is something to narrow it down a bit so you can make a selection from a few choice companies.

If you're typical of Wall Street newcomers, chances are you'll start by writing to as many brokers as you can, asking them to put you on their mailing list for research studies and recommendations.

This is good because, if nothing else, it serves to bring the whole picture into sharper focus. The research, for the most part, is honest and the conclusions are honestly reached.

A broker is not in business to drive you out of the stock market. His purpose is to persuade you to invest. Therefore he doesn't analyze a company and tell you *not* to buy its stock. If he thinks a company's stock should not be bought, he won't waste the expense of analysis. He'll simply ignore it.

So you must remember that anything a broker analyzes and recommends is to encourage you to buy that stock. Even if you take your brokerage business to another firm, he's still happy, for your purchase of the stock will help support the market in it, and the regular customers who followed his advice will be pleased. Moreover, chances are that he has a position in the stock himself.

There's nothing wrong with this procedure. You don't want to know the companies in which you should *not* invest. You are only interested in the ones the experts think you should put your money into.

Even if you've contacted only half a dozen brokers, you'll find your mail filled with suggestions. Upon arraying the analyses and recommendations, you will be dismayed to see that there is still an enormous smorgasbord of goodies, appearing all the more succulent from the descriptions in the reports.

You'll notice that many of these reports are so forthright that they even recommend at what price to buy a stock and at what price to sell it.

(A little voice should tell you that a good stock isn't a good investment one month and a poor investment the next. The *buy and sell* advice is for traders—those who go into a stock for a gain and then sell it when the rise is believed at its end. A really good stock —the kind you want—should weather the selling of the traders and move forward on its own, providing the kind of activity more pleasing to *investors* such as yourself, than to traders. But you'll have to check such facts with your broker; maybe that good stock is only good for a few points' gain.)

Perhaps, at this time, you decide to subscribe to some professional literature. Highly recommended for a man searching for a stock to invest in is the *Wall Street Transcript*, an expensive weekly trade paper selling at six dollars a copy or $210 annually.

Its value to you is that it prints, *in toto*, all the research reports of the leading brokerage houses in New York, and scores from around the country. But here again, you'll be confronted with the smorgasbord, and as a novice, you may find the array of morsels too bewildering.

You may have decided, of course, just how you want to diversify your portfolio. Perhaps you want a good food chain, an automotive company, a sturdy utility, and something in electronics. Or you may want an aerospace company, a financial company, plus something a bit daring in the computer field.

Even then, you're faced with the basic problem: How do you select one good food chain out of the many offered on this laden board? Or one automotive stock? Or one utility?

At about this time you are tempted to buy some kind of professional help.

If you have one hundred thousand dollars or more to invest it is possible to retain one of the many excellent investment counselors who, for a service fee, will take the problem off your hands. Some will do it with as little as twenty-five thousand dollars to invest, but most have higher limits.

The records of some counselors have been impressive. Customarily they handle large trusts and big estates, giant pension funds and the like, and are simply not geared to handle a small account of a few thousand or a few tens of thousands. Some bank trust departments will handle *common trusts* under certain conditions, and if you put in as little as thirty-five thousand dollars, they will add your money to a common fund and invest the whole in one portfolio.

Another device is to subscribe to one of the many *advisory services*. They operate in a controversial area of the stock market, with many vocal fans and many vociferous detractors.

Looking at the advisory services, again there is a smorgasbord. Some offer a wide variety of aids for the small investor. Some specialize in particular services. Some offer statistical information. Some prepare charts. Some provide recommendations about hundreds of stocks and make recommendations about what to buy, what to sell and what to hold. Some review and forecast business conditions as they are believed to affect the market. Some comment solely on the national economy. Some offer technical forecasts of the stock market itself.

A few do provide a form of individualized service for the small investor, and for a negotiated fee will handle his investments, or at least provide him with personalized recommendations so he can handle them himself. The bottom limit is about twenty-five thousand dollars for the portfolio.

It seems to me that the decision to retain or not to retain an advisor or counselor separates the men from the boys in the stock market.

The *men* learn to stand on their own, supported by their selected financial and statistical aids, and they render their own decisions. To them accrues the enormous satisfaction of seeing their own portfolios grow and enrich over the years, knowing that every decision, good or bad, that affected it, was their own. It is only a matter of time before most decisions are good ones.

What are the statistical aids mentioned in the preceding paragraph?

Unless you wish to acquire an expensive library, basic statistical information must come from your broker. He will have on file the volumes of the three basic research and advisory services. These are:

Standard & Poor's Corporation
Moody's Investors Service
Fitch Investors Service

In volumes called Standard & Poor's *Corporation Records* and Moody's *Manuals*, you will find most of the basic research material you need to make your market decisions. Most brokerage offices have customers' rooms where you may take the volume you want from the broker's reference library and copy down your own research. The two massive sets, containing tens of thousands of pages, carry statistical histories of every publicly owned corporation in the country and full financial data covering a period of years.

The big set, Standard & Poor's *Corporation Records* comes in six big looseleaf volumes in which reports of companies are arranged in alphabetical order. These reports contain all the basic financial data. Whenever a new annual report is issued or important developments are announced, substitute looseleaf pages are inserted.

Moody's *Manuals* come in five volumes:

Industrials
Railroads
Utilities
Banks and Finance
Municipal Bonds

Fitch publishes a semi-annual and an annual *Forecast* which is also found in most broker's reference rooms. In a bound volume there you'll also find Fitch's *Weekly Survey*, an eight-page market letter.

Both Standard & Poor's and Moody's have the special services and market letters that are also found in brokerage houses to assist you in basic research on a particular company, or on industrial trends in the marketplace.

Fitch's *Stock Record* and Standard & Poor's *Stock Guide* are issued monthly. They, too, are useful to the individual investor. (Anyone wishing to subscribe to such services as the *Stock Guide* or *Stock Record*, will find that they are not expensive and, when interpreted properly, can be worth the cost.)

Let's clarify a point here. It is not necessary for the individual investor to spend hours in the reference room of his broker's office, and to go around with ink-stained fingers while he records the doings of the companies that interest him.

Your *registered representative*—the man you'll deal with in your broker's office—will dig out all the facts you want and supply them to you readily. Chances are, he'll have them at his fingertips, and can present them to you on short notice.

But it is necessary for you to know what you're looking for, and to know where the information comes from, so the wisest thing to do is to visit your broker's office and familiarize yourself with all three of the major reference and research services. Look up *your* companies in all three, and see how they are treated, statistically and factually.

The primary research involves a company's figures for assets, income, earnings, dividends and debt, all in relation to stock prices, and all going back over a period of years.

For experimental purposes, select a company in which you're interested, go to your broker's office, ask to be directed to the reference room and look up these figures. Perhaps you can get your registered representative to help the first time. There's a trick to it, of course, and it takes patience. It is surprising that many veteran investors still don't know how to look up a corporation's record in Standard & Poor's cumulative index.

Don't become one of them. Know what you want in the way of information from your registered representative, and be familiar with his sources of information. That way you're not dependent on him. Not all registered reps respond with the alacrity that you might wish, and further, in this day of great mobility, you may be dealing with a half-dozen registered representatives in a variety of spots around the country.

But all of this still hasn't put you into the stock market. You still haven't bought any stock, because you have yet to make a decision about what securities to buy.

And the truth is, as you now recognize, you're simply not ready.

When you realize this truth, and if you plan to do something about it, here's a recommendation for you.

For the first year, hire a competent, reputable investment advisory service.

It need be neither elaborate nor costly.

Standard & Poor's, for instance, offers a program built around one of its publications, *Investment Advisory Survey*. For a sixty-five dollar annual fee you receive its eight-page confidential bulletin, featuring a supervised list of recommended investments, with inquiry and consultation service. For one hundred dollars, the same organization offers a *Portfolio Review Service*, which provides analysis of the subscribers' holdings, full inquiry privileges, and individualized specific recommendations on what to buy, sell or hold.

Moody's *Investors Advisory Service* offers subscribers a review of their existing holdings plus constant supervision of their portfolio through up-to-date reports, with specific recommendations (to buy, sell or hold). For this the agency charges $184 per year for a portfolio of fifteen stocks or less, and two dollars for each additional stock.

Fitch's, too, offers an investment advisory service, and though the author has had no personal experience with it, it is said to be fine, and not too expensive.

By and large the records show that if you stick with an investment advisory service, your portfolio will turn in a performance about on par with the Dow Jones Industrial Average. If the averages gain six points in one year, so, likely, will your portfolio. If they drop six, you may see the drop reflected in your portfolio.

From the standpoint of the novice, however, an investment advisory service may be useful for getting started in the stock market. For a relatively painless fee you can buy top-notch expert supervision for your own portfolio, for a short period of time.

By the end of a year you will have learned enough to be able to intelligently challenge some of the decisions that have been made in your behalf. Moreover, if you think as I do, you may regard your portfolio in a different light, looking at it with long-range binoculars, rather than with a trader's eyes.

By then, you'll be an investor.

Meantime, here are some addresses that may be of use to you:

> Fitch Investors Service
> 120 Wall Street
> New York, N.Y. 10005
>
> Moody's Investors Service
> 99 Church Street
> New York, N.Y. 10007
>
> Standard & Poor's Corporation
> 345 Hudson Street
> New York, N.Y. 10014

VIII *The Broker—*
A Doctor or a Merchant?

It is surprising how many small investors get less than wholehearted cooperation from their brokers when it comes to getting information about a corporation or an industry. No answer, or a curt one, is often the only reply an innocent investor receives. What causes this grumpy attitude on the part of the professional broker, who, after all, should be ready to help his customers?

Most of the time this response results from an incorrect approach. What you are seeking, really, is not information but *advice*. Brokers are loath to give specific advice to a client for an obvious reason—they can be wrong. This is particularly true when they don't control what you do in acting on the advice. And they're in line to be blamed if anything goes wrong. They have learned that one bit of advice requires another bit at a later time. If they advise on the "right time to buy," they must also be allowed to advise on the "right time to sell."

The way *not* to treat a broker is to ask him for flat advice on whether to buy a certain stock. If it happens to be a security that his firm is currently interested in, and on which it has just completed research, then you may get a definite answer. Otherwise, you're not likely to.

So don't ask for advice—ask for information.

First you must learn *how* to ask for information, so you'll get what you want.

The proper way to get maximum use from your broker's reference library and research department is to ask him, or his registered representative, specific questions. That way you'll get responses that are accurate and should be useful to you. You, however, will be obliged to make the ultimate decision as to whether you buy the security that has interested you.

Your broker should be glad to help you interpret the facts and figures that he has garnered for you.

Any broker who has a reference library and a good research department—and these days most of them do have and all of them should have—will be glad to dig out any information you request, if you are a client, and will do it for a small fee if you're not. Very often, the large *wire houses*—brokerages with offices in many cities —will assemble good research for you at no charge even if you're not a client, in the hope that you will become one. But under such circumstances don't look for professional interpretation. It is better to pay a small fee and get some expert's view of the material at hand.

A broker will consider it a waste of his time and yours to embark on a vague mission of research. If you know what you're doing, your query will be specific, asking for facts that are in the records.

The best way is to state exactly what you're looking for:

"Look, Mr. Broker, I've been interested in buying stock in Chucklehead Mills Corporation, but I've read about some drastic management changes lately. On the other hand, I've read where they have a new double-knit process that sounds promising.

"If they can make knitted men's garments as well as they make double-knitted women's dresses, it seems likely that it will open up profitable new markets for the manufacturer.

"What I need to know is:

"1. Quality of the present management.
"2. Status of its current production, both the type and method.
"3. Condition of its markets.
"4. Status of its competitors.
"5. Latest financial statements."

It sounds like a titanic order. It isn't, because the broker, knowing that you need this information in order to reach a decision about buying the stock, has all the facts on file or knows where to get them.

In a few days' time you could normally expect to receive from your broker a *research package* that typically might contain the following:

1. Chucklehead Mills Corporation's report to stockholders on the appointment of Melvin G. Flynn as president and chief executive officer, together with his qualifications and the Board of Directors' reasons for wanting him in the top slot. Along with this would be comments on the calibre of senior executives serving immediately under Mr. Flynn. (The report will not say so, right out, but it should strongly indicate that the Board of Directors has wisely set up a chain of command that can quickly become a chain of succession in the event anything should happen to Mr. Flynn.)

2. A research department report that will give an account of Chucklehead Mills' new double-knit process that bodes well to revolutionize garment textile manufacturing.

This will deal not only with the method of production, but with the profit potential for Chucklehead, and will give a good rundown on the market for this double-knit product, and the comparative position of Chucklehead's principal competitors.

Very likely the report will include other appraisals and opinions, such as a statement from a leading garment manufacturer who buys his fabrics from Chucklehead Mills, or one by a fashion designer, who comments on the potential acceptability of clothes made from double-knit fabric.

The report, or sections of it, may not be new. It may be from a previous compilation made by the research department, perhaps for someone else, perhaps for its own edification. Unless it is very old, however, its information should be regarded as valid. A two-or-three month span of time in the corporate world is regarded as "current" for, because of size, the corporate process is burdensome and slow.

3. The *financials*, which should include the balance sheet and statement of profit and loss from the latest annual report, plus the latest "interim" or quarterly report, should complete the package.

Armed with this information, you should be well on your way toward making a decision about whether or not to buy Chucklehead Mills Corporation's common stock.

However, you may need some interpretation of the material you have received.

If you do, your registered representative in the broker's office should be glad to oblige. If he isn't helpful in this area, he's not doing his job, and you should feel justified in looking elsewhere.

In fact, if you don't receive as much information as described in our imaginary research package, you may need a new broker.

For the truth is, you can't possibly make a valid decision on whether or not to buy Chucklehead Mills without the information sketched out in the foregoing. Indeed, a wise investor would want additional information before going ahead.

Your broker, incidentally, should be listed as a member of the New York Stock Exchange and of the American Stock Exchange. This means that he has an additional set of hard and fast rules governing his ethics and behavior, along with those tough ones laid down by the Securities and Exchange Commission in the wake of the debacle of the 1920's. Those rules are there for your protection.

It's also important that a *member firm* of the New York Stock Exchange has access to additional services that are advantageous to you. A broker who is a member of the New York Stock Exchange has his own traders on the trading floor of the Exchange. This means that your order can be executed virtually under the direct control and supervision of your own registered representative.

A member firm also has ready access to the Stock Exchange Quotation Bureau and can get you a last-minute quote on any stock that's listed at any time.

There are some good brokerage firms that are not members of the New York Stock Exchange—that is, they do not own a *seat* on the Exchange—but you should be a wise and seasoned investor before dealing with them in buying stocks that are listed on the Exchange. Why not take all the service and all the protection you can get, especially when you're starting out?

Bear in mind that, in the final analysis, the only really acceptable answer to the question of which stock to buy is one you must work out for yourself through investigation and study. You should find most of the solution in the research package that you get from your broker.

If there remain some specific things you think you should know, try asking the broker again for those specific answers. He'll accommodate you.

Just how valuable is the advice you can get from a broker? After all, a broker is interested in selling securities. He's not likely to pass out bad or depressing information about securities, is he?

Yes, he is, if there's bad news to be found.

He's not interested in selling that security alone. He has hundreds of them available to sell, good ones that are not likely to disappoint a client. Far more important than selling a security is the survival of his business. He can't last long without satisfied clients.

His income is based solely on the commissions he charges for buying stock for you. It doesn't make much difference to him *which* stock it is, for the commissions are just about the same. If you have one thousand dollars to invest in one security or another, he'll get about the same commission no matter what your decisions may be. His transcending interest is to see that you invest wisely so that you'll be happy and will come back to him when you want to trade, switch, sell or buy.

This may not be quite the case if you're thinking about over-the-counter stocks—which you shouldn't be, if you're a novice. Over-the-counter stocks are not listed on either of the big exchanges. In the OTC market, commissions may be more flexible, and a broker who is obliged to protect his own investment in an over-the-counter stock by *making a market* in it, may be tempted to do a little huckstering. Even so, he knows that in the long haul this is not good business practice, and a big, legitimate brokerage firm should be expected to avoid such dealings.

Generally speaking, however, your broker or registered representative doesn't particularly care which of the Big Board stocks you purchase—just so long as you do buy some securities, and you are happy with them.

And, also generally speaking, you can trust your broker or registered representative to do right by you.

Looking at it candidly, your broker is the best qualified person to help you. He knows much more about the stock market than your banker, your lawyer, and your accountant, though each on his own may be regarded as a wise and successful investor—and he's certainly better qualified than the fellows you meet for lunch or have a drink with at the club.

Your registered representative spends about forty hours a week working in, or brooding over, the specialized field of securities. The facts and figures needed to help you to reach a decision are at his fingertips. He has access to Standard & Poor's *Corporation Records* and to Moody's *Manuals*. Backing this up, usually, is his own research department, trained to dig out the information most needed in making a market decision.

The research department may be the key. If your broker doesn't have one, or doesn't have a *good* one, you may not be getting your money's worth.

Not infrequently the registered representative and the research department may appear to be in conflict, and this is good, for it helps you to make a good decision.

"What?" asks the registered representative. "You want to buy Webbfoot Railroad? Well, I wouldn't. Railroads in general are in for a bad winter."

Then the research department, having been queried, writes: "Steel mills will be operating at capacity during the next six months, and all industries connected with it should share in the prosperity, including those in the transportation category (trucks, rails, ships) that move limestone, coal, iron ore, ingots or bars."

"Well, wait a minute," the registered representative says, "this might very well apply to Webbfoot Railroad. As I recall, it's deeply involved in the steel business. Let's check Research again and see what they come up with."

Sure enough, the research department discloses that Webbfoot Railroad does fifteen percent of its business in coal hauling; thirty-one percent in hauling limestone; and twenty-nine percent in moving ingots and bars. That means that seventy-five percent of its income is derived from the steel industry which, the earlier advisory disclosed, will be booming.

"On the basis of this," the registered representative now says, "you might take another good look at Webbfoot Railroad. Of course, there are other things you should know, but it's worth your time to look it up. I'll get the information for you."

A good research department is the heart of a good brokerage firm. A well-functioning research department keeps track of all the new developments affecting the corporations whose securities are traded on the exchanges, and of news that might affect the securities themselves, or the stock market itself. Researchers read dozens of business, industrial and economic publications, plus scores of trade and technical periodicals, and file the information so that it is readily retrievable as it is needed.

Researchers inspect the facilities of corporations they monitor, and keep in touch with management through periodic interviews. They also subscribe to some of the key advisory services to make certain they don't miss anything about a corporation under their surveillance.

Blended into this vast flow of information are special advisories about the industries, the economy and the market as it relates to the specific industries into which the separate corporations fit.

It is the duty of the researchers to issue a steady flow of reports on numerous industries and separate corporations. Those reports that are prepared in depth are frequently offered to the public, sometimes at a nominal charge for non-clients. See the advertising on the financial pages of your newspaper for a guide to what is currently offered. Other reports, usually briefer, are for the information and guidance of the registered representatives.

A word here about the registered representative. He's the man you'll most likely be dealing with when you call your broker. In the '20's he was known as a customers' man. In those days he was loosely regulated and was usually an active trader in the market himself. Sometimes with only nebulous authorization he would buy or sell for a client's account without first contacting the client. As a result of the market crash of October 24, 1929, he got a bad name.

At some point in the '30's or '40's when the Securities and Exchange Commission and the New York Stock Exchange were "cleaning up" all previous bad practices in the stock market, the customers' man became known as the registered representative.

The word registered means that he is, in effect, licensed by the New York Stock Exchange. He is qualified after passing a tough and penetrating examination following attendance at required training sessions.

The word representative means that he represents both you, the client, and the broker. While, loosely speaking, he is a broker, the real broker is the man who owns the brokerage firm, or the partners who own it. Today, since brokerage firms can incorporate (they could not do so until a few years ago), the top corporate officers are seldom brokers, *per se*, but more often administrators of the business.

How much help you get from your broker in making investment decisions depends on you—and, of course, on how his own facilities stack up, particularly his research department.

You cannot—and should not—rely on him to make any ultimate decision. That must be yours.

The broker will not accept complete discretionary authority, as with power-of-attorney, except under unusual circumstances. He might do it temporarily, if you are an old and valued client and you want for example, to make a safari to Africa. Even then, you'd have to make out a strong case.

He would rather airlift a research package to you in Africa and have you make your own decision, and then let him know about it.

He will act on your specific instructions and buy or sell as you direct, and you can trust him to get you the best price either way.

If he's a good registered representative, he'll supply you with all the information you need to make that decision wisely, and will make interpretations as requested.

Then it's up to you.

IX *How to Get the Most Out of Your Broker*

No group of American businessmen is as dedicated to missionary work as stock brokers, the *registered representatives* of Wall Street firms. With fervor and zeal they spread the word, believing almost religiously that the ownership of common stocks serves the highest purpose of the capitalistic system.

They will tell you that it creates millions of part-owners of hundreds of businesses operating under the free enterprise system. It pools private wealth for the creation of new companies and whole new industries. It rewards thrift. And, it compensates the hard-working who dig for facts and information.

The pooling of investment capital, they will tell you, creates the millions of jobs that make America rich, and engenders the competitive system that provides opportunity to those who seek to climb to the top.

Nowhere else on earth is the ownership of common stock equated quite so closely with Godliness and Patriotism as it is in America. This is due largely to the disciples of the brokerage firms who spread wide and far the Teachings of the Gospel according to the New York Stock Exchange.

To prove that they are true missionaries, brokers eagerly await invitations to speak at investment clubs where, even if they land the club's commission business, the profits are dismally small.

Let it be a clue to all who serve on entertainment committees of local investment clubs and other organizations, that stock brokers are the most available speakers one can find. And many of them, strangely enough, are keenly interesting. This is particularly true if they have had any experience in a research department and know how to apply analysis to a corporation or an industry.

Many brokers even know how to apply this knowledge when it comes to giving advice about an individual's investments, though it must be remembered that many do not.

To pass the test and become a registered representative, a broker must learn many things. Nothing among them, however, has to do with properly researching a corporation's common stock or the techniques and tricks of managing an individual portfolio. The broker's training is basically in how to buy or sell a share of stock, or a million shares of stock, in the stock market. It is up to the customer to order what he buys and sells.

Since any broker who is duly registered can buy or sell any listed share of stock for you, many brokers strive to give some semblance of personalized service as a bonus to their customers, in the hope that they may retain their business.

This takes the form of informal counseling, and frequently involves giving specific advice.

This can be a bit tricky, and what you ask for, and what you get involves some subtleties.

For instance, if you ask your broker what he thinks of Lymphatic Lamp, he'll most likely give you the latest quarterly report and whatever research report he has in his file. He'll supply information, but not an opinion.

On the other hand if you ask him a direct question, like, "Should I buy Lymphatic Lamp?" he's likely to do one of two things: 1) either give it some serious thought before advising you about the stock, or, 2) merely tell you that it seems okay to him.

A good way to test the calibre of your broker is to ask him for a direct opinion about a specific stock, telling him that you wish to buy it if he thinks it is a good buy.

If your broker goes so far as to say something like, "Lymphatic Lamp looks all right to me, but I wouldn't sell anything I own in order to buy it," it means he is giving up two commissions—a sale and a purchase—so you *know* he's giving advice that is in your interest, not his.

I became a loyal customer of a broker who advised me not to buy a certain medium-priced stock about which I had heard a rumor and on which I had done a little research.

I was all set to buy it, but I asked him to check it and two days later he called me and advised me not to buy.

It turned out that he was wrong. The stock enjoyed a rather spectacular gain during the ensuing months. On several occasions my broker told me how badly he felt about giving me poor advice.

But that wasn't the point at all. He took the trouble to look up the stock and to analyze it (or have his research department to it), and in the expert judgment it was not a good buy.

The broker's opinion was better-founded than mine, which was based mostly on rumor. (The rumor involved a pending merger and it could have gone either way.) Thus, if I had bought it on the strength of the rumor and it had turned out to be a profitable move, it would still have been due to luck rather than research.

In the long haul, I decided, it was better to have a broker who cared sufficiently to turn down a certain commission and run the risk of my ire by giving me what he thought was good advice.

That broker, who is still at the old stand in Wall Street today, will remember the incident when he reads this, and I'm sure he still feels badly about the advice. However, for my money, he's one of the best brokers in the business.

The perils of the discretionary account were outlined in the preceding chapter, and while an unscrupulous broker can benefit by having your power-of-attorney, and an ethical one may succeed in making you some profit, the average broker does not want discretionary power over your account, and will avoid it if possible. He prefers to have you give him orders—orders to sell or to buy specific stocks. That's what he's geared to handle best.

He draws a fine line between *information* and *advice*.

If you ask him how such-and-such a company is doing, he'll dig out all the information he has at hand and give it to you so that you can analyze it and make up your mind about the stock.

If you ask him point-blank if he thinks you should buy the stock, he'd like to duck the question, and may do so.

Just as you may make a wrong decision about a stock, so may your broker, and so may his expert in the research department, who is supposed to be thoroughly familiar with the stock you inquire about. Knowing that there's a chance he may give poor advice, the broker, as much as possible, avoids giving it.

Basically, though, advice is the keystone of his business.

Some brokers charge a modest fee for doing research on a stock in your behalf and advising you about it. This way they feel justified in spending more time on it and have less fear about expressing an opinion on whether you should buy, sell or switch.

Brokers do not advertise such services, and you will have to inquire of your own whether he's geared to handle you or not.

Most of the larger brokerage firms, and a majority of them *are* large these days (since the small ones have a hard time surviving in their highly competitive field), have their own research departments wherein labor a variety of experts who have familiarized themselves with particular aspects of the economy.

For instance there may be a researcher who heads the petroleum department. It is his responsibility to be completely familiar with the oil industry, ranging from geological surveys and exploration, to transportation, the pipelines, refining, marketing and research. He has to know the corporate composition of every company in that industry, be familiar with those which have incurred debts, which have undergone management changes, which have brought out new products, which have overextended in plant and equipment.

There are experts of this calibre for each industry and for many sub-industries (such as medical and drug supplies, for instance), as well as experts on the various types and varieties of bonds.

Chances are that Lymphatic Lamp would be considered in the electrical fixture and appliance industry and there would be a researcher in the brokerage house who knew all about it—if such a company as Lymphatic Lamp really existed.

When a researcher analyzes a company, he digs into all of its facets. He analyzes its markets, its competitors, its productive capacity, its production methods, its plant and equipment, its financial structure, its management, its research facilities, the personnel in research, the calibre of its sales force, and many other factors.

After a report is prepared on a specific company, the research department sometimes condenses it and puts it into a special report for customers. Sometimes this is in pamphlet form, or it may be only two or three mimeographed pages.

If it's brand new and if it's "hot," the broker usually advertises it. The financial section of the Sunday papers is his favorite spot for this. Sometimes he puts a modest price tag on it for non-customers, to help defray the cost of the research. Customers usually get a copy of the report mailed to them free of charge.

Now, if you are a customer of a brokerage firm that had a research report in its files on Lymphatic Lamp, and if you inquired about it, you probably would receive a copy of that report plus the latest interim report—that, and nothing else.

You would be obliged to read the report and perhaps ask for reports of competitors of Lymphatic Lamp, and then make up your own mind as to whether or not you wanted to buy the stock.

For a price—usually a flat fee based on the size of your portfolio —you can ask for advice from your broker on Lymphatic Lamp or any other stock.

This is well worth the small cost to you. It is highly recommended as a matter of wise procedure. This way, you can initiate the ideas but allow the final decision to be made by the experts. While your broker as a registered representative does not, himself, pretend to be an expert in managing a portfolio, he has access, through his firm, to persons who are both qualified and capable.

If you hire counseling from your broker's staff, you may be told that Lymphatic Lamp looks all right, but that you should also consider General Electric, Westinghouse and Sylvania if you want to get into the electrical fixtures and appliances field. At face value this is worthless information, unless you pin your adviser down and ask him which one *he* would buy. Implicit in such a report, however, is the suggestion that the researcher believes there are better buys in that field than Lymphatic Lamp.

Another phrase in such a report that always throws this writer is: *in its price range*, such as, "Lymphatic Lamp seems a good buy *in its price range.*"

What the researcher usually means is that if you buy Lymphatic Lamp at some figure near its present price, it will be a satisfactory purchase. It has a double meaning, however, which lets him off the hook. It can also mean that he thinks you'll do better to buy a more expensive stock. Perhaps General Electric at twice the price of Lymphatic Lamp is something that will give you twice the value. Perhaps the researcher means that with your available cash you should buy fifty shares of General Electric rather than one hundred shares of Lymphatic Lamp.

This is the time to ask blunt questions. Get a direct answer from the researcher, so you'll know where you stand.

If you have a good customer relationship with your broker, perhaps cemented by the fact that you are purchasing some counseling service from him, you may be in line to benefit from special reports emanating from his research department. He might notify you in *advance* that a very favorable report is about to be released on a specific corporation, thus permitting you to buy the stock before the general public finds it attractive and bids up its price.

He cannot do this if there is "new" information in the report —something that never before has been published or made public.

With that kind of information he has to keep the report secret until it can be released to the general public.

Most of the time, however, a report contains nothing new, but can, and on many occasions does, shed a whole new light on a company.

Many venerable companies have been "discovered" by the research department of a brokerage house or investment advisory firm. A classic example is American Telephone & Telegraph. For years "Ma Bell" was considered good, grey and dull, until the analysts discovered that it was worthy of any investor's attention.

If a research report like this is under preparation in your broker-age firm, there is nothing unethical involved if your broker tips you off to the fact that the report is about ready to be released, and suggests that you might want to buy some of the stock before the general public gets onto it.

It's done all the time.

One sure way to make certain that you are kept posted on what the research department is doing is to insist that you be put on the mailing list for everything that comes out of the department. It is information that you should have for your own files, anyway.

Don't expect your broker to act in your behalf unless he does have power-of-attorney over your discretionary account. No broker will put you into or sell you out of any stock without your specific orders.

The men and women who work in research departments are human beings who, like the rest of us, respond to certain other people. If you do your own research thoroughly, if you keep yourself well-informed, you will find rapport with the researchers in your brokerage firm, and you can benefit from their expertise.

There's nothing more that a researcher enjoys discussing than research. If he finds you're well-grounded and know what you're doing, he'll probably open up and tell you things that you ought to know, and dig out some facts that will help you.

Generally speaking, you can't barge into the research depart-ment of your broker's office and ask to see the man who handles electrical appliances and fixtures.

Researchers are generally kept segregated from the public, first so they may do their work without distractions, and second, because the brokerage is set up so you'll deal primarily with the salesmen or registered representatives.

But after your association with the firm has been established and you have dealt with one researcher or another, perhaps through their reports, and possibly by letter, they'll get to know who you are, and you can get the kind of help you want.

If you were buying real estate several times a year, you'd not only know your broker, you'd be very familiar with his appraisers, construction men, mortgage man, and lawyer.

When it comes to your stock broker, don't settle for dealing exclusively with your registered representative. Get to know what goes on in the research department, and become acquainted with the people in it.

X How to Use "Insider's Information"

Experience shows that far too many investors, particularly newcomers to the marketplace, rely on "tips" and "inside information," and base their investment judgments on such tidbits of gossip or rumor.

Hard-nosed skeptics and cynics who mistrust their own doctor's advice and who ignore the counsel of their lawyers will place implicit faith in the investment "tips" of the clerk who prepares their chocolate ice cream sodas.

They will seek out people who work in Wall Street or those who are employed in branch offices of brokerage firms in the belief that proximity even to the paperwork of the stock market brings not only sagacious insight into its functions but access to information that is not available to the average person.

When I was Business and Financial Editor of the *New York Herald Tribune,* one of my best sources for tips was the man who ran the shoeshine stand I patronized. Knowing my affiliation with Wall Street he confided inside information to me in the vain hope that I would reciprocate. I always listened to his tips, because they amused me. Most of them came out of market letters or advisories that were available to anyone. Some even came out of the newspapers which, because of my job, I had to read thoroughly every day.

His tips, however, were as good as any you could get anywhere.

There exists, of course, genuine inside information. A top corporate executive does know more about his own company than the average investor can learn. If he has any common sense he must have a very good idea of what company activities will influence the price of his stock, either up or down.

For competitive reasons, however, he does not chat openly about these activities or plans. He wouldn't hold his position long if he did. Moreover, he is forbidden by law from disclosing any information that affects the stock of his company. If he should confide any information of value to a member of a stock brokerage firm who uses it to his own advantage or to the advantage of his clients—even just *one* client—the broker will be suspended from trading and probably fined as well by the Securities and Exchange Commission.

Protecting you in this world of insider's information is the *full-disclosure* law. No information may be given out to anyone, this law states, unless it is given to *all* who may be concerned—and that includes the general public. There is an additional regulation that makes it necessary for a corporate officer to make full disclosure of his own market trading to the SEC.

When a researcher from a brokerage firm begins to dig into the affairs of a corporation, his firm usually forbids him to deal in the stock of that company until his report is made public. He may do an exhaustive study of the company and present a detailed report to his superiors, but they, too, are restrained from trading in the stock for their own accounts until the report has been made public.

The information garnered by the researcher in time becomes a market report or an advisory and is sent to all of the clients of the brokerage house for which he works, either as an inducement to buy or a suggestion to sell that stock. Sometimes it advises owners to hold the stock for the time being.

At the same time it is offered to the general public, sometimes free of charge, sometimes for a fee. You'll see notice of these reports advertised in the financial pages of your newspaper, especially on Sundays.

Customarily the researcher is an expert in a specific field. He keeps abreast of developments in a whole industry and of doings in each corporation in that industry. Thus the researcher for a major

broker who studies the Penn Central Railroad is likely to be an
expert in the affairs of the entire railroad industry. This way he can
see a corporation in its proper perspective and can make comparisons
between the figures and functions of a specific corporation and the
averages and trends in the whole industry within which it operates.

There are some strictly Wall Street publications that also prepare research for their readers. These include *Barron's*, the *Wall
Street Transcript*, *Forbes' Magazine*, *Financial World*, *Wall Street
Reports*, *Business Week*, *Investment Dealer's Digest*, and others.
The *Wall Street Journal*, of course, a bible for many investors, is in
a class by itself. It does not attempt to research or analyze specific
corporations, but to the student of the market and regular reader,
it is a storehouse of valuable information.

The news of companies, corporations and industries is vital to
the investor when he makes his investment decision, but such information bears only obliquely on the performance of the market itself.

"How's the market doing?" you'll hear people ask many times
in the course of the working day in Wall Street. They are not
inquiring about a specific stock, but about the market as a whole.

"Up two and one-half," will be the reply.

This means that the Dow-Jones Industrial Average of thirty
stocks (a composite index) has advanced by two dollars and fifty
cents.

Your particular stock may not be in the thirty that are measured
and weighted in the Dow-Jones index, but the report gives you a
fairly accurate idea of how the stock market itself is doing in broad
terms.

There have been times, of course, when the Dow-Jones Industrial Average has advanced when many of the other stocks have
declined, and vice versa, but generally speaking the Dow is an accurate reflection of what's going on. Its figures are posted regularly
throughout the trading day, so that at 11:30 in the morning you can
see at a glance how the market was doing at 11 A.M.

The Dow-Jones Company is a private corporation, parent of

the *Wall Street Journal, Barron's* and other publications, and the statistical compilation of its averages is a major function. Great care is taken to see that the prices are weighted to accurately reflect the crests and ebbs of the market in the averages.

The way to find out what the market is really doing, and how individual stocks fared, is to consult a daily newspaper. Morning newspapers usually carry the complete transactions of the New York Stock Exchange, the American Stock Exchange, the National Exchange, and some Over-the-Counter quotations. Many evening newspapers, except those on the West Coast, go to press too early to accommodate closing quotations. Some use 2:30 P.M. prices. Those with "Late" editions can give you closing prices for the same day.

If you have difficulty getting the information you wish in your local newspaper, the *Wall Street Journal,* which is available in the early morning in all parts of the country, and the *New York Times,* which is available in larger cities and resorts throughout the country, carry all the information you need. Their lists are accurate, complete, and contain final closing prices.

It is of value to you as an investor to know what the market is doing, though unless you're a heavy investor, or make trading your full-time occupation, it's not necessary to keep track of the hourly movements of the price list. A check with your morning paper each day should keep you sufficiently posted.

It is good to know how the market is doing, for you will want to make your own decisions based on the current trends.

As to *why* the market does what it does, you might just as well pick your favorite expert and rely on his explanation. Accept it at face value, for it is likely to be as accurate as anyone else's.

In the Spring and Summer of 1970 when the market dropped severely, there was no valid reason for it, but hundreds of learned reasons for it were committed to eternal records. When the market rose rapidly and set new peaks in the Fall and Winter of 1970–71, again copious explanations were written. In truth there was no valid reason for the powerful rise, other than the mood and disposition of the buying public.

What is a share of common stock worth? Its market value is simply what someone is willing to pay for it when you're ready to sell it. That's its value—that, and nothing else. It has two other values in a technical sense, though they mean little to the average trader. One is *par* value, that is the price at which the stock was first issued. The other is *book* value, which is roughly the value of the share if the company should be liquidated. A bad management or a good management can change the book value of a stock in short order.

Essentially, however, you're interested in the market price for your stock. The market price is quoted in the stock tables of your newspaper.

You'll find the stocks listed alphabetically. Let's pretend that our favorite stock, Lymphatic Lamp, is listed on the New York Stock Exchange (though in reality, it is not sufficiently capitalized even to be traded officially as an over-the-counter stock). You'll note that it, like all others, is abbreviated. It is listed as *Lym Lmp.*

This abbreviation is not to be confused with the stock symbol that is assigned to Lymphatic Lamp by the Exchange for purposes of posting its price. That would be, let's say, LLX, and that's how it is listed at the Exchange and on the ticker tape that is used in brokerage offices throughout the world. In a board room you would watch the tape (projected onto an illuminated strip) until you saw the symbol LLX, and then the next two figures would reveal what had happened in the latest trade. The first figure would be the price of the last trade, and the second figure would be the amount of change from the previous trade, if any.

In your newspaper stock tables, abbreviations are used rather than symbols, because to follow the entire list, a reader would have to refer back to his symbol book for each item. Such a book will be given to you by your broker, or you can get one by writing to the Stock Exchange.

Here's how the newspaper shows Lymphatic Lamp:

Year to Date		Stock &	Sales in					Net
High	Low	Dividend	100's	Open	High	Low	Close	Change
22½	18¼	Lym Lmp(.25)	20	21½	22½	21½	22½	+1

Now, what does this one line of type tell you?

I have made it a habit to look at the year's high first and then at the close and net change.

Following this method with Lymphatic Lamp you see that it set a new high for the year in yesterday's session, when it closed at 22½. The net change shows you that it advanced one point over the previous close.

After the abbreviated name, Lym Lmp, you notice in parentheses the figure .25. As a stockholder, you really don't need this information, but it is of value to some other traders who do not already own Lym Lmp. It reports that Lymphatic Lamp has declared a regularly quarterly dividend of .25. You will recall that your dividend notice said that the dividend would be payable on such-and-such a date to stockholders of record on such-and-such a date. This dividend announcement will appear in the newspaper until four trading days before the record date, when it will be dropped until the next dividend period.

You will also want to check the stock's activity. The 20 indicates that twenty hundred shares (or two thousand shares) were sold yesterday.

Then follows the record of yesterday's trading. The first sale was for 21½. The low was exactly the same as the first sale. The close set the high for the day.

The owner of Lymphatic Lamp could look at that account of yesterday's performance and feel quite comfortable. It was a good healthy advance. There were no wide fluctuations in the price of the stock. Lym Lmp seems to be doing all right. It has been traded in a very narrow range all year, and now, maybe, it's on its way up.

A glance through the rest of the list will show you that the stocks that are generally regarded as being of investment quality, or investment type, are also traded in a rather narrow range. Those with the wide fluctuations recorded both for the year to date and for the daily activity, are regarded as more speculative.

At the bottom of the stock tables is a very complicated-appearing "box" set in small type that contains all of the information relating to footnotes. When you encounter a footnote in any part of the quotation that you're interested in, be sure to look up its meaning at the end of the table. This can give you information about dividends, extra dividends, skipped dividends, or stock dividends, among many other things.

There is one thing in your quotation that will fool you if you're not careful. The net change (it's $+1$ for Lym Lmp) is the change in the closing price from one day to the next. It is not the difference between the opening and closing prices, nor is it the difference between the high and the low. Obviously yesterday's close was 21½, the same as the opening bid today. With the close at 22½, the gain was one point.

Let's go back to the dividend for a moment. We recall that Lymphatic Lamp directors declared the dividend payable, let's say, March 10 to stockholders "of record" of February 22. On four trading days before the record date, or February 19 (if no Saturdays, Sundays or holidays intervene), the stock *goes ex-dividend*, and the quotation will note this. That is because it requires four trading days to transfer stock and enter the owner's name in the company's records. Obviously anyone buying the stock February 19 can't be on the company's record books on February 22, so he will miss the dividend. It will go to the previous owner.

It is expected that the price of the stock will drop by the amount of the dividend. In this case it is twenty-five cents or 1/4 point. Therefore if there is a drop of 1/4 in the trading on February 19, it will not show in the net change. That will remain unchanged but after the listing of the name of the stock will be the notation "ex-div."

The same procedure applies to rights (or are you one of the ones who calls them warrants?). It requires four days to transfer and record stock whether it involves rights or dividends or anything else, so that four days before the expiration date of a right, the listing will note "ex-rts."

It would be foolish, indeed, to try to make a judgment about a stock by looking at its listing for one day, but if you watch it in the daily paper for any period of time, you will get an idea of its performance, and this, coupled with the research that you will do on it if you're truly interested, will provide you with much of the information that you need.

If you have a favorite stock that you're watching and it doesn't appear in the list in your newspaper on a certain day, it may mean that there was no trading in your stock on that day. You can then turn to the "Bid and Asked" list in your newspaper to get its latest quotations. Not all newspapers carry this, but the larger ones do. Both the *Wall Street Journal* and the *New York Times* carry "Bid and Asked" quotations.

Many people don't realize it, but even on a very active day there may be no trading at all in as many as four or five hundred of the fourteen hundred stocks traded on the Big Board.

American Stock Exchange listings are treated in exactly the same manner as the New York Stock Exchange's, although in some of the smaller cities the newspapers do not print all the Amex quotes.

When it comes to Over-The-Counter quotations and the listings of the Regional Exchanges, local editors make their own rules and in large measure it depends on how much local demand there is for a specific quotation.

Even the New York City newspapers do not carry anywhere near the full list of Over-the-Counter quotations, and that includes the *Times* and *Wall Street Journal.* These lists, fuller in the *Times* and *Journal* than anywhere else, are reviewed and revised constantly, and only those stocks with the greatest amount of activity and keenest interest among traders are quoted.

No quotation is added to the OTC list unless it is requested in writing by a reliable person or firm, and even that is no guarantee that the newspapers will print it.

XI How Not to Be a Speculator

Until the day that someone sings *Nearer My God To Thee* over your recumbent figure, you will be a speculator of great stature. This is not a fortune or a forecast, it is a fact. Life, itself, is one giant speculation. So is work or a job, where nothing is ever certain. The mere possession of money in itself is speculation of high order, for you never know whether it will purchase more or less when you get around to spending it.

Every decision you make involves speculation. Drive downtown or walk? If you drive you lose valuable exercise. If you walk, you may be drenched with rain before you get home. You speculate on which to do.

Every boss is a speculator each time he hires someone or assigns a task.

Every farmer is a speculator when he tosses a seed toward the ground, for you simply can't depend on nature.

Every housewife speculates when she adds a dash of salt to something she's cooking.

On the grim side, every pedestrian at a street corner is a speculator. So is every driver behind a wheel of a car.

It has always amused me to hear new investors come to Wall Street, their savings all dolled up and waiting to be put into the market, and say to their brokers, "I don't want to speculate, I want to invest."

Not speculate? Good grief! After speculating on everything all their lives, they come to the one place that is geared up to handle speculation properly, legally and fairly, and they say they don't want to speculate. It's about the only place in the world where you can speculate with most of the odds rigged in your favor.

What they mean is that they don't want to gamble.

In truth, they *do* want to speculate—they just haven't reasoned it out.

Gambling involves nothing but chance. It revolves on the spin of a wheel, the turn of a card, the cast of some dice, the flip of a coin, the pace of a horse or the drawing of a lot.

Speculation involves hard work—research, the assembling of facts, the application of logic and the exercise of reason.

There is risk in gambling, and the odds have been worked out for those who are addicted.

There is less risk in *speculating* than in almost anything you can do, if you have done your homework and are speculating knowledgably.

When you say, "I would rather invest than speculate," you don't really mean it. What you truly mean is that you would rather speculate than gamble.

Banks invest. They buy *investments*. Trust accounts buy *investments*. Conservatively managed custodial funds (pension funds and the like) buy *investments*. Tightly-governed insurance companies buy *investments*.

They invest millions, sometimes hundreds of millions in securities that yield them comparatively small return because there is no speculative factor in them. They are as much as any securities can possibly be, Gibraltar-like in their steadfastness, but penurious in their payout.

Individuals, unless they are rich enough to be considered in the institution class by themselves, buy *securities*. They do not buy *investments*. Securities are speculative.

You, unless you're uncommonly fortunate in the money department, will buy securities, not investments, and therefore you will be called upon to speculate.

We are not quibbling over the meaning of a word. There *is* a vast technical difference.

The word *investments* is technically applied in Wall Street *only* to government bonds, good municipal bonds and the highest-quality corporate bonds. It does not include common stocks.

When you're dealing with someone else's money in a custodial capacity, it is necessary to follow a course set out under what is called the *Prudent Man Rule*, in which you sacrifice some earning power for safety. Thus the conservative buyer of securities for a bank may spend his working day trading in the gilt-edged world of governments and municipals, but spend his evenings at home figuring out what he wants to add to his personal portfolio in the way of common stocks. As a professional he cannot speculate; as an individual, he wants to.

A *bond* carries a commitment to repay its face value on a specific date, and to pay a certain rate of interest in the interim. This gives it the safety that the custodial manager needs in order to protect himself as he invests other people's money.

A common stock, of course, carries no such guarantee. It can rise in value, it can decline in value. Its directors will vote dividends in accordance with their own corporate rules, based upon their current earnings and their company's future prospects.

This, in the strict sense of the word, makes a corporate stock a risk to its owner. It is a risk in that it may not increase in value as much as you thought it would. It is a risk in that you may not receive the dividend that you expected.

When a wise man buys securities, however, he doesn't have to do so on the basis of sheer chance. He has every opportunity to do a little research on a company and then make an intelligent assessment of the risk he will take in buying that company's stock. If a company has paid dividends, say, for fifty years without skipping once, it hardly seems a wild risk to buy some of it's common stock if it is now performing as it has in the past and if its current price is right. You shouldn't be in for too many surprises, particularly if you buy to hold, and do not consider yourself an in-and-out trader.

There are other ways to avoid being a reckless speculator.

You, as a non-trader, should probably content yourself at the outset of your venture into Wall Street with what are considered to be *investment-type* stocks. Remember, no common stocks can be regarded as legitimate investments, technically, so we are discussing that select group of securities that has shown itself to be so stable that even the investment community refers to them as investment-type stocks.

The first thing you should ask of your registered representative is to prepare you a list of some good investment-type stocks so you can be studying them.

These will probably be the securities of the leading companies in such industries as utilities, banking, chemicals, foods, food processors, and financial institutions.

The list changes from time to time as one corporation or another drops from special grace. And remember, please, that just because utilities are listed, it doesn't mean that all utilities merit the special blessing. This is, indeed, a select list. In the grading of risk, *per se*, these rank just under legitimate investment-grade bonds. Their dividends, though steady and sure, may not be so attractive.

Traders—the legitimate kind who make their fortunes buying and selling securities—know that there is a wide variety of stocks rated just below the topflight securities that pay extremely liberal dividends to attract investors, because they are *cyclical.*

This means that the fortunes of these companies are more directly tied in with the general business cycle, and rise and fall with it. Cyclical securities include those of many companies in many industries. For example, there are those in the steel, automobile, construction, railroad and clothing industries.

Professional traders ride these stocks through their ups and downs, hold them until the good dividend is declared, and perhaps get out until the next quarter rolls around.

As a non-trader, you would buy such stocks to hold, and would get the benefit of the higher-than-ordinary dividend, while ignoring the fluctuations of the cyclical market.

Actually you have one of four objectives in your purchase of common stocks:

1. Securities that pay steady dividends.
2. Securities that pay liberal dividends.
3. Good quality stocks that will increase in value in the years ahead.
4. Attractive speculations.

Encompassed in those four objectives is an extraordinary amount of latitude.

We have explored the investment-type stocks and the cyclical stocks.

The first meet Objective No. 1—securities that pay steady dividends.

The second meet Objective No. 2—securities that pay liberal dividends, but not always so steadily.

The cyclical stocks are from the middle-ground of risk-taking. They are shares of good and reliable companies geared to the rise and fall of business cycles. It is not as blatant as in the old days when you'd buy Bangor & Aroostock Railroad on the report of a bumper potato crop in Maine, but a large segment of the corporate world does, indeed, finds its fortunes directly tied to specific cycles.

Let's cite a simple example. When money and credit are scarce, buyers of new cars take out thirty-six-month notes with their banks and finance companies, rather than the twenty-four-month notes that call for stiffer monthly payments. Thus a second-year "lull" can be expected in the new car market, seriously affecting the profits of automobile companies for that year.

Hence the stocks of automobile manufacturers become predictably cyclical and their market value can be expected to reflect the periodic assessments of the experts.

Because these corporations must protect their own treasury stock and the value of their titanic investments, they customarily pay higher-than-average dividends to attract market support through the downside of their cycles.

Many times the degree of risk can be measured by the generosity of the dividends, though this is not always the case. Don't get carried away with the dream of high dividends in the cyclicals, however—just remember there are many people still around who thought you could never lose money on Studebaker stock, even though it had its cyclical ups and downs. Studebaker paid dividends for more than fifty years.

What are the stocks of Objective No. 3? They are, of course, the *good growth stocks*. These are not to be confused with the many hundreds of stocks that are also growth stocks but fall into category No. 4—*attractive speculations*.

Perhaps the hardest to locate are the *good growth stocks*. They are the securities of companies that often pay small dividends or none at all, and are regarded as attractive because of their future prospects for success.

Some companies—chemicals, for example—require many years to build up their own energy as they develop laboratory prowess to match growing markets. Would you believe that not too long ago the august E. I. du Pont de Nemours & Company was regarded as a "good growth situation"?

Others may be infant industries, such as electronics, a few years back, or nuclear industries, more recently, or cyrogenetics, even more recently.

Only recently graduated from the good growth situations are stocks of companies in aviation, natural gas, computers, data processing, air conditioning, pharmaceuticals, and, of course, electronics. Back in the '30's, automobile manufacturers and radio broadcasters were regarded as good growth stocks.

Investing in some of these companies in years gone by did require a degree of risk, and the stocks, of course, were speculative, to say the least. But again, research must have shown that if the company in the growth industry met certain conditions, it had a good chance to be successful.

These conditions are basic. They apply to any company whose stock is for sale. They require that a company be:

1. Sufficiently financed.
2. Competently managed.
3. Alert to developments in its industry (preferably ahead of them).

Some of the finest automobiles ever built were produced in the 1920's, but neither the cars nor companies are around any more, simply because management wasn't alert to rapid developments in the industry. Their stocks were regarded as either good growth situations, or attractive speculations.

Those basic conditions should be your guide as you look to the growth stocks of the future. Some companies, in any industry, will survive and prosper and become giants. Others won't. In fact, most won't. The failure almost always can be traced to inadequate financing, incompetent management or ineptitude in regard to industry developments. Frequently there is some degree of all three faults.

The point is, they are discernible in advance.

If a company has to keep going to the well for more financing, there's something wrong, unless the need can be traced directly to capital investment in plant, equipment, material, design or sales staff, to meet growing demands.

If a corporation doesn't keep up with other companies in the industry as far as profits and earnings are concerned, there's something wrong.

If a company lacks verve, and if its executives are involved in a high turnover rate, there's something wrong with management.

If a company is lagging behind in developments that open new markets, there's something wrong.

There is ample opportunity to check on these factors before you buy, and to keep track afterwards. They are simple guidelines and should be used periodically for measurement on every security you own, or plan to.

If you read in the *Wall Street Journal* that a company whose stock you own has just elected a new chief executive officer, read the account in full to find out what you can of his background, and then write to the finance officer of the company and ask to be informed what's going on. It would also be a good idea to call your registered representative at the broker's office and ask him about it. Chances are, he'll know. There are official management watchers in every good brokerage house who are well-apprised of the careers of the professional managers.

If you spot a piece in the *New York Times* that says such-and-such a company is ready to market a thingamabob, the same thingamabob that your company has been working on as a development project, get on the phone to your registered representative and ask for a report. You have reason to believe the competition is getting the upper hand and perhaps that's where your money should be invested.

Don't be too jittery, and don't challenge every bit of news that you see. And don't sit back and demand that there be a constant flow of good-news press releases about your company. Judge your own company by the things you observe and read about other companies in the same category and in the same industry.

On the other hand, if you read nothing about your company but its annual report and interim reports, you may have occasion to be worried, and it would be prudent to take a closer look at it. Any living, breathing company makes news of one sort or another over a period of time.

There are some *special situation* securities among the growth stocks that someone may try to interest you in. If you are exceedingly well-advised, and under the guidance of a good solid professional, they may merit your attention.

These are the speculative securities of companies that have been *depressed* for one reason or another. The future looks good, not because it is so rosy, but because it appears a great deal better than the past.

Corporations are virtually living beings and they do not always succumb to their illnesses. It is possible to survive a period of bad management, or to recover from a series of tough breaks, or to come forward with a technical breakthrough after years of barely getting along with mediocre earnings.

If a professional spots a good company with a bad record that is showing signs of recovery, he has a *long-shot speculation.* Long shot it is, and it must be so regarded, but many handsome profits have been turned by buying the depressed bonds of such a company and collecting all the interest payments that had been deferred during the bad times. The same is true, of course, of preferred stock with deferred dividends. It, too, is a *long-shot speculation,* and is bought at a depressed price in the hope that the deferred dividends will one day be paid to the owners of the stock.

If you really want to gamble, and many staid businessmen like to reserve a small portion of their investment portfolios for "throwing the dice on Wall Street," there are the *penny stocks.*

These are usually the securities of new ventures—the fellow with the better mouse trap, the man with oil leases right next to J. Paul Getty's gusher, the chap with the gadget that will make the color television tube obsolete.

The professional advisers all counsel staying away from the penny stocks because they have a bad record as a group.

I don't say that. Not at all. Venture capital is the essence of our entire economic system. If you have an adequate portfolio, and if you're in a tax bracket where you can take a little loss, it's not only fun to gamble, it's helpful to the economy. Go ahead with a little risk. It's bargain day in the basement, and who knows, you might track down a real goody.

Both electronics and data processing brought forth a rash of new enterprises that started out as penny stocks and have now either been merged into giant conglomerates or are standing with the leaders all by themselves, much to the enrichment of the gamblers who took a fling on them when they were first issued.

There is great pleasure, I am told, in being rich, and there is much enjoyment in making a good, big profit, but in many respects penny stocks provide the fun side of Wall Street and the stock market. After wading through the research on an IBM, it's relaxing to throw a few dollars to the wind and see what happens to them. For many, it has more allure than turf or table.

Gambling is a luxury, however. Gambling can be fun or it can be a curse.

It is better to own one share of IBM after you researched it, than a thousand shares of penny stocks.

Only after your regular portfolio has been built up through proper methods and is adequately diversified, should you even consider the penny shares—and then it should be done sparingly, knowingly, and gingerly.

After finishing a hard job of work, you're entitled to some fun, but don't overdo it.

XII *Your Partner, the Tax Man*

We have shown in the preceding chapter that everyone is a speculator unless he is investing in government or municipal bonds or
treasury notes.

This holds true until you come into contact with your ever-
present partner in Wall Street, the gentleman from the Internal
Revenue Service who wants twenty-five percent of what you earn on
a capital gains basis with your trades, and more, if you operate on
a short-term basis. His presence makes short-term traders, ergo
speculators—out of people who normally would be investors.

Hate to even read about taxes? Well, you'd better prepare to
plod on, for the tax factor is the most important one that governs
a large portion of stock market activity.

Tax considerations will play a dominant role in every move you
make in Wall Street—if you're lucky. Simply, if you're an unsuccessful investor, you won't be fretting about taxes, except how to realize
a loss and carry it forward to other income. If you're a successful
investor, you'll not only worry about taxes, you'll find yourself doing
your trading to conform with tax requirements, for your own benefit.

On this basis, a speculator is a man who puts his money in the
market with a view toward a quick-term profit. The investor, therefore, is the one who puts his money to work by buying ownership
in a company, expecting to earn a reasonable and regular return over
the long haul.

The speculator is not interested in dividends. He is interested
in a rise in price on his stock, making a quick profit, and getting his
money out fast.

Under the Federal tax laws, he will be able to keep more of that
money than he would if he had received the same amount in salary,

dividends, or any other kind of income, short of income produced from a business of his own.

Thus you might start out being an *investor*, fully intending to invest for the long haul, and wind up becoming a *speculator* in order to save money on taxes. It's a happy circumstance, and it occurs all of the time.

The reason is, of course, the *capital gains tax.*

Risk capital is the most essential ingredient in the economic growth of America. If it were not for risk capital, there could be little, if any, progress: no homes, no office buildings, no industrial plants; no cars, no television sets, no mass-produced clothes or shoes; no foods, no medicines, no processed or packaged or canned goods; no trains, planes, ships or buses.

Realizing the importance of risk capital, Congress has gone to great pains to keep it flowing. One such way is to give special tax treatment to profits realized by risking one's capital. These profits are called capital gains, and they include the profits realized on the purchase and sale of securities, for the money you advance to purchase securities in a company enables that company to expand or do its thing, whatever it is.

The law provides that a man who makes a profit on any security that he has owned for more than six months—that profit being called a *long-term capital gain*—will not have to pay a tax of more than twenty-five percent of that profit.

That twenty-five percent is the maximum. If a taxpayer is in the millionaire class, and pays ninety-one percent tax on personal income, he will still pay only twenty-five percent on his long-term capital gains.

If the taxpayer is in the lower income bracket and is taxed at only twenty percent, he can absorb his gains as personal income and pay only twenty percent on them.

On the other hand, *short-term capital gains*—that is, profits realized on the sale of securities held for less than six months—are taxed at regular income tax rates, depending on the taxpayer's individual bracket.

It is apparent that the wealthier you are, the more attractive you will find the idea of stock speculation with its twenty-five percent long-term capital gains features. The higher your tax bracket, the more drawn you are to the idea of a twenty-five percent maximum tax on long-term capital gains.

There are additional advantages in long-term capital gains situations. Losses may be used to offset gains, and may be carried forward to offset future gains. A speculator who realizes ten thousand dollars profit on one transaction, but who loses five thousand dollars on another, pays a tax on only five thousand dollars, the tax at the rate of twenty-five percent.

If the deal goes the other way—if he loses ten thousand dollars in one transaction and earns a profit of five thousand dollars in another—he pays no tax at all on the five thousand dollars profit, and has an additional five thousand dollars long-term capital loss to carry forward and apply against future profits.

To put icing on this cake, the government even allows him to deduct a maximum of one thousand dollars a year of whatever losses he may suffer from his *other* income, thus reducing his regular tax. He must be involved in a capital gains situation in order to get this added benefit.

This is, unquestionably, favored tax treatment. If there are those who feel that it is a loophole, and fear that it may be plugged one day, they should be heartened by the opinion of the majority of economists, who believe that the long-term capital gains concession is *not enough,* and urge the government to make far greater concessions to the speculators.

They want to shorten the time required to qualify for the long-term capital gains tax rate, or to eliminate the time requirement altogether. Others argue that the rate should be reduced below the twenty-five percent figure. Many fast-growing countries have no capital gains requirement whatsoever.

They cite the need for a great flow of venture capital to American business to finance its enormous progress, and say that it should be much more freely available.

With a little imagination you can see how the capital gains tax, even in its present form, could affect you under certain circumstances, turning you from a sober investor into an overnight speculator.

Let's say that a certain stock you bought at fifty dollars a share, because you thought it an attractive investment with a record of good dividends and a history of reliable progress, suddenly caught the attention of the speculators and the market price increased to one hundred dollars a share.

You face two choices:

1. You can remain an *investor*, ignore the price rise and take your normal dividend, which you will have to count as personal income, applying to your individual tax bracket.

2. You can become an instant *speculator*, and sell out, taking a one hundred percent profit (minus commissions, of course) on which you know you have to pay a tax of no more than twenty-five percent.

Such a move on your part is predicated on two factors:

1. That your income bracket is such that it is worth your while to sell out and take a long-term capital gains profit.

2. That you have every reason to believe the price rise in your stock is speculative and will not hold at one hundred dollars for long, but will slip back toward the price at which you purchased it.

If you believe the price rise is genuine and warranted by viable and durable market support and it will remain in the neighborhood of one hundred dollars, all present market conditions considered, you may be making an unwise move to sell just for capital gains, since you could do so at any time in the future that it suited your purpose.

And this, you can see, is what separates the absolute speculator from the investor-speculator.

The real speculator doesn't care a bit about the long-range prospects for your stock or any other one. His concern is with current market price and the prospects of a particular stock over the next six months.

It does him no good, under most usual circumstances, if a stock reaches its peak three months after he buys it and he has to sell quickly for a short-term capital gain. The short-term profit becomes personal income, and in his bracket, it could be costly.

This has led to development of a syndrome in Wall Street known as *Six-Month-Vision.* A great many professional traders have learned to their sorrow that they missed out on some fine investments because they failed to observe the long-range prospects and limited their quest to a six-to-eight month gain.

There's a flip side to this coin, and it also has its sorrowing souls. Too much concern about paying the capital gains tax leads many an investor to hold on too long. He refuses to sell and take a profit because he'll have to pay a short-term capital gains tax on it. He calls this being *locked in.* It's an expression you'll hear often in market circles.

While he grumbles about it, the market dwindles, and he loses his profit.

There are experts in Wall Street who say that this fear of the capital gains tax costs stockholders hundreds of millions in profits each year.

It seems inconsistent to tell a person to be a long-term investor on the one hand and then, on the other, advise him that there are are likely to be times when he should become a speculator.

It is only common sense, however, when you have enjoyed a wholesome profit from a stock, to reconcile yourself to paying a capital gains tax on it and taking it out of your portfolio. It's a pity, but it is a fact, a fact based in the Internal Revenue Code. For if you hold onto a stock that has enhanced in value to a considerable extent, and if you are lucky enough to keep the profit, you are merely postponing the day of reckoning. If you postpone it until the day you die, you will merely pass the tax burden along to your heirs and executors.

It's a paradox, that capital gains tax. By its very nature it breeds speculation. It offers the man of high income a chance to build up

capital at a bargain tax rate. On the other hand it dampens speculation among amateurs and the poorly advised, because they fall prey
to that most human of frailties, the desire to postpone paying a tax
as long as possible.

As long as a capital gain can be offset by a capital loss, there
will be those who can avoid payment of even the capital gains tax.
A man with a capital gain will be encouraged to take a greater-than-
ordinary risk because of the knowledge that if he loses, Uncle Sam
will cover his losses—at least to the extent of twenty-five percent of
the capital gain.

The purpose of this chapter is not to encourage you to become
a speculator. A professional speculator, as we shall see, is a keenly
knowledgable trader with his finger on many pulses. Like you, he
gambles on his own judgment, and bets against the mass movements
in the market by anticipating them.

Rather, the purpose is to show you that there are times when
it pays you to be a speculator, and there will be times when you
should, in your own interest, act as one. Most of the time, however,
the non-professional should think of himself as an investor whose
portfolio is structured for the long haul.

Let's clear up an additional point about the professional
speculator. Rarely does he buy truly speculative stocks.

Instead he does his speculating on the most active stocks on the
list, most of which are the securities of front-ranking corporations.
These *most actives* account for the majority of the transactions on
the New York Stock Exchange.

He buys for one of two reasons, because he thinks the market
itself is too low, or he thinks the price of a particular stock is too low.

His judgment in each case is based on deep study.

He may study the stock of a company from top to bottom and
decide that the price is either too low right now, or that it is more
than likely to rise in the future. If this stock is on the most active
lists it means that the price fairly represents the combined judgment
of all the people who are buying and selling.

With his intimate knowledge of the stock, he then pits his judgment against the public judgment, by buying it, hoping to hold it for six months and then sell at a profit.

On the same basis, the professional speculator may feel that he has a better grasp of the market than the general public, and he buys his securities speculating that the market will be different in six months' time.

Of course, this is not always predicated on a rising market. He may believe that a special security will sell lower, or he may be convinced that in six months' time the market will be trending downward. In this case he sells short—but that's a different story that we will tackle in the next chapter.

There are numerous devices for protecting profits made from speculation, even the inadvertent speculation that might occur to you, the long-range investor. We will explore these devices in subsequent chapters, for, hopefully, you'll have to use them.

Just about the nicest thing that could happen to any long-range investor is to have his portfolio become so valuable because of the high market price of his stocks that he has to resort to devices to protect his profits.

If you make your choices wisely, if you've learned your lessons well, there is good reason to believe that before long, you'll be facing those happy problems, and using the professionals' devices to conserve your winnings.

And that *isn't* gambling.

XIII *How and When to Sell It Short*

In the days following the great stock market crash of 1929, many prominent citizens were publicly castigated in the press and elsewhere because they had made money, while others lost it, by *selling short* during the decline. Somehow there was a connotation of evildoing, if only because selling short was an expression of lack of faith in the Red, White and Blue All-American Stock Market. It was regarded as an unpatriotic act, if not a greater crime.

The same misunderstanding persists today, nearly a half-century later.

Though it accounts for only a small percentage of the transactions on the New York Stock Exchange, short selling embodies an evil excitement about it, and its sinister practitioners, modern reincarnations of "Bet A Million" Gates, Jay Gould and others of their kind are regarded as market insiders who burrow around looking for weak spots, the way the twenty-four-hour flu bug assails the intestines.

Yet short selling is a very ethical, practical and even necessary function, which may come to your rescue one day if you are forced to speculate by market conditions beyond your control.

A short sale is simply the reverse of the usual market transaction.

Instead of buying a stock and then selling it, as in the customary practice, the short trader sells it first and then promises to buy it back —at what he hopes will be a lower price.

On the surface it seems arguable to say that if you can buy a stock because you think it's going to go up, it's just as reasonable to sell it because you think it's going to go down. Your object is to make a profit. Why shouldn't you be able to make it in either direction, up or down? There's room here for the Right Thinkers to contend that the rights of the bear who wants to sell short are just as valid as those of the bull who wants to buy long. Above it all is the transcending marketing principle that for every buyer there must be a seller, and vice versa.

The weakness lies in the fact that the public believes you shouldn't be able to sell something you don't have. When some short seller was *caught short* by having the market rise instead of decline as he had expected and found he didn't have enough money to buy back the higher priced stock on the delivery date, Daniel Drew was alleged to have quipped:

> "He who sells what isn't his'n,
> Must buy it back or go to prison."

And that, of course, is the truth, the harsh truth facing all short traders. It is stronger medicine than that applied to dozens of other business transactions when a trader promises to deliver something that he doesn't own at the time he makes the sale.

Almost every commodity that we consume is traded on a future market where a farmer pledges to deliver so many bushels or pounds of a certain grain or vegetable on a specific date, and receives payment in advance on the signing of a contract. He is selling something that he doesn't yet possess.

So is every bond-issuer. He pledges to pay money on a certain date, but at the time of the issuance of the bond he usually doesn't have the money to pay. He is selling money that he doesn't own.

To be technical about it, the short seller really isn't selling something that he doesn't have. He *borrows* the stock that he sells, and he has to give it back to the lender. He hopes to buy it back at a price less than he sold it for. He calls this *covering*. He covers his short sale, making a profit.

Again, theory looks good on paper but turns out somewhat differently in practice. Who would want to lend stock to a short trader so *he* can sell it at what he regards to be the top of the market for that stock? Certainly not the people who bought it in expectation that it would rise, for implicit in the sale is the repurchase of the stock at a specific date.

He borrows it from his broker, who lends it from a margin account where he has previously worked out a lending agreement with his margin customer. (This is standard practice when opening a margin account, as explained in the next chapter.)

If the broker doesn't have the specific stock that his short seller wants to borrow, he shops around among other brokers until he gets it, then *he*—the broker—*buys* it, on a temporary basis, from the other broker, and lends it to his short trader, who sells it.

The other broker is willing to sell because he has temporary but free use of the money until the stock is returned. If that particular stock is in brisk demand—as may be the case if it's reaching toward its peak—the second broker may demand a premium for lending it, and this is charged against the short seller. If the stock continues to rise, he may call for additional premium. If the price begins to drop, however, the borrowing broker will most likely demand a proportionate refund.

The same rules that apply to margin buying cover the short seller. If the Federal Reserve Board has a fifty percent margin rule in force, the short seller must put up cash equal to fifty percent of the market value of the stock that he borrows and then sells. Under rules of the New York Stock Exchange the minimum margin cannot be less than one thousand dollars.

Suppose you wanted to sell short one hundred shares of stock whose current market price was 50. If the margin requirement was fifty percent, you'd have to put up fifty percent of the purchase price, or $2,500.

If the stock dropped to 40, you could buy it back for four thousand dollars. You would cover your short position by returning the stock, at which time your $1,500 margin would be credited to your account. You would have made a profit of ten dollars a share, or one thousand dollars less taxes and commissions.

But who says the stock will stop falling at 40? The short seller suspects that the stock is enroute to a lower price level. He can make more money by hanging onto the stock while its price drops. Yet there's always the nagging question that instead it may rise.

Under these circumstances the short seller protects his position by placing a stop order to buy at one point above the market price where he would normally sell. In this case, with the market at 40, he would place a *stop order* to buy at 41. This way, if the market turns and the price begins to rise, his stop order becomes a market order to buy as soon as the stock hits 41. At that price his profit will be nine hundred dollars, minus commissions and taxes.

The short seller isn't obliged under the rules to buy back a stock in the event of a *rise* in market price. However, he would get an automatic call for more margin. For this reason, short sellers are obliged to keep a larger supply of cash in their margin accounts than are regular margin traders.

If the stock selling for 50 rose to 55, for instance, his original margin would be inadequate. He had already put up fifty percent cash for stock costing five thousand dollars, or a margin of $2,500. But the stock is now worth $5,500, so he will get a call for more margin. He has the option, of course, to take his loss and buy the stock at 55 and close out the deal.

This, too, is done, by even the smartest of the short traders.

To prevent wrongdoing, which we shall explore in a moment, the Securities and Exchange Commission has a hard and fast rule requiring that stock be sold short only on a rising market. This is called selling on the *up tick*.

The order to sell, as it goes to the floor broker on the trading floor of the stock exchange, is clearly stamped or marked, SHORT SALE. The floor broker is forbidden to sell the stock except at a higher price than the last sale price of the stock. Thus, in the case of our short seller, if he saw the stock reach 40, and put in a bid to buy at 40, the stock could not be purchased by him except at 40 ⅛.

The one exception to this rule would be if the stock had dropped below 39⅞ and the last previous sale price had been 39 ⅞, indicating a rising trend, then the short seller's bid could be executed at 40. This is called buying on an *even tick*.

Why all this upticking and eventicking?

It is to prevent people from forcing a stock's price down by manipulative means in order to make profitable short sales. Now a stock's price has to show some signs of recovery before the short trader can complete his transaction. If a stock continues to decline, he simply can't buy it back. He has to withdraw his order to buy and enter new ones as the stock drops.

All of this safeguarding is a result of the exploits of the old pool operators and the great, fearsome Moguls in Wall Street in the old days.

The way to win the game in those days was to get a corner on the stock of a company—that is, to hold so much of it that those with short sales couldn't buy the stock to pay back because there was none to be had. Since they were obliged, under law, to buy it back, those holding the corner could dictate the terms. They could set a price on the stock that was exorbitant, ruining the speculators who had been on the short side.

The most famous case of this kind—it's called the Classic Corner—involved the Harlem Railroad, predecessor of the New York Central (now the Penn-Central). (The Harlem Division of the Penn Central is the old Harlem Railroad.)

Commodore William H. Vanderbilt got control of the Harlem and extended the railroad from its Bronx terminus down through Manhattan. Daniel Drew, a notorious stock trader, was a stockholder in the railroad and had realized a good profit as Vanderbilt proceeded with his plans and the price of the stock advanced sharply.

Drew sensed a chance to make a much larger profit. He induced some cronies on the New York City Council to repeal the franchise that had been granted for extension of the railroad. He and his pals then sold the stock short.

That blatant maneuver forced the price of the stock downward, and Drew and his friends on the Council rubbed their hands in glee.

There was only one thing wrong. They had underestimated Vanderbilt. As Drew and his friends sold, the Commodore was buying.

When it was all over, Drew and his associates on the City Council found that they had sold more stock than really existed. This, in anybody's court, is a crime.

They could not cover their short positions except on the terms dictated by Commodore Vanderbilt. Needless to say, the terms were disastrous, and wiped out Drew, along with his less-affluent friends on the Council.

Other short sellers who used to be in the market but are banned today are directors and officers of corporations who sometimes acted on inside information to trade in their own company's stock. Both officers and directors are forbidden from making short sales in their company's stock today. Officers cannot sell stock in their company for a profit unless they hold it for six months.

Referring back to the operations of the speculator in relation to the investor in Chapter XI, you can see where there might come a time when you, an old sober-sided investor-for-the-long-haul, might suddenly want to become not only a speculator but a short-trader to boot.

Suppose that cherished industrial stock of yours has been hanging in at around 85 for a year or more, adding an average of a couple of points gain each year, when it suddenly catches fire and soars up to 100. Investigation shows you that the reason for the rise is that it has become a most active stock. The public is buying it. It has been discovered. These things happen.

If you're sure of what you're doing, it is worth your while to make a capital gains sale. Unload at 100 to the mob that has suddenly found glamour in your stock. It's sensible to sell, even though you may have to give up twenty-five percent of your profit to Uncle Sam.

Normally, the thing to do would be to sell the stock and forget it, and start searching for something else to substitute.

However, for a variety of reasons, you may decide you really like that stock, and while you feel compelled to sell it, you really wish you didn't have to.

Providing that you're sure the price rise is nothing more than temporary public adulation, you may follow up your transaction with a short sale, buying it back at 85, leaving you just about where you started.

You'll be where you started as far as your portfolio is concerned, but you'll have pocketed profit on both sides of the move—on its rise and on the stock's subsequent decline.

This is not recommended procedure, but you may feel yourself forced to do it at some point. It's not unusual for some portfolio-builder to find himself in such an unexpected squeeze. It's a happy circumstance, and a profitable exercise.

The key, obviously, is in being certain that the excitement over your stock is not really justified and is occasioned only by temporary public support.

In moving away from a situation in which the general public thinks your stock is good, you will be practicing the science of contrary thinking—its art was explored in earlier chapters.

Don't follow the public.

XIV *Margin Yourself into Debt*

The mere word margin is dangerous. It smacks of royal blue tycoonery. It conjures up ambitious pictures of great profits and the legendary figures who built empires in the Wall Street of bygone days.

Margin was the vehicle that carried poor men to mountains of riches in the 1920's, turning paupers into multi-millionaires in a short period of time. It was also the elevator that slipped its cable and plummeted many into the armies of penniless vagabonds of the 1930's. As one of the bubbles in the froth of innocence and foam of skulduggery that filled the financial world in those days, it was a major contributor to the great market crash of 1929 and to the great depression that followed.

Margin is again respectable today, and a useful tool to the stock trader. It is scrupulously monitored, both by the Federal Reserve Board and by individual brokers operating under the tight regulations of the New York Stock Exchange. It is still a high-voltage device and can be handled safely only by those who know all there is to know about it.

Margin is instant debt. Don't even think of it unless you can afford to go into debt deeper than you are at present. As a matter of fact, even if you think you want a margin account and apply for one, your broker may not let you use margin unless he is thoroughly satisfied that you *can* pay the debt—immediately and on call, without notice.

A security buyer must assure his broker (and sometimes the

broker's banker, too) of his financial responsibility before he can open an account.

Once he does, he can buy stocks by making a down payment on them. He can trade cheap stocks for expensive ones, like trading up for a more expensive model car. In a rising market he can enjoy much larger profits than his fellow traders who do not use margin.

Many new doors are opened to the margin trader. Behind some of them, however, lurk financial pitfalls that can be painful and costly. Aware, and alert to their dangers, the average trader can utilize margin very profitably as a speculator. He can find it a life-saver for even a stabilized portfolio, as described in Chapter XIII, for it will allow him to sell short without going through a lot of red tape. For if it does nothing else, a margin account gives him a good credit rating with his broker.

Margin is not for everyone. It is only for the trader who has been very successful or is affluent anyway, for it takes high stakes to make the game worth the effort and risk.

The New York Stock Exchange regulation requires that the security buyer's share of a margin trade be for at least one thousand dollars.

Then, in addition, brokers have their own rules. Most will not allow a customer to buy stock on margin unless it sells for at least three dollars a share. With some it may be five dollars a share or even higher.

On top of this is the *margin requirement,* a minimum percentage figure for downpayment set by the Federal Reserve Board, which is ordered by Congress to regulate margin.

You can see that you must be in sound financial shape to consider buying on margin. Chalk it up to another example of the indisputable adage: "Them as has, gits."

The Federal Reserve Board is required by Congress to state exactly what the margin requirement will be at any given time. It does this by making it mandatory to pay a certain percentage of the total value of the stock that is bought on margin. The Board changes this margin requirement from time to time, depending on how apprehensive it is about inflation (when it tightens up on everything that it can), and how much stock trading is being done on margin. When it fears the pressures of inflation, the Fed raises margin requirements, as it has done in recent years. For this reason it has not been too worried about the amount of margin activity, since a high margin requirement tends to automatically keep margin trading down.

The Federal Reserve Board was charged with responsibility for margin requirement in 1934, as one of a rash of new laws designed to clean up the financial community following the big crash in 1929. The lowest figure the board has ever set was forty percent from 1937 to 1945. The highest was one hundred percent that was ordered from January 1946 to February 1947 when postwar inflation threatened the economy. That meant there was no margin at all—one had to put up one hundred percent to buy stock.

Most of the time the rate is set between fifty percent and seventy-five percent—a far cry from the margins set by the brokers themselves in the 1920's when, if you were known to people in a brokerage house, you could get as low as ten percent margin, and almost anybody could get twenty percent margin.

Let's suppose that the margin requirement is fifty percent when you decide to buy on margin. There is a listed stock selling for twenty-five dollars and you happen to have about $2,500 in spare cash that you'd like to invest. (Note: unlisted Amex or O-T-C stocks cannot be bought on margin.) Ordinarily you would buy one hundred shares of that twenty-five dollar stock with your $2,500, but this time you feel certain that your selection is going to rise by several points over the coming year or so. As a result you feel confident that you can make a margin trade and come out ahead.

Because the margin requirement is fifty percent, you use your $2,500 as down payment on two hundred shares (rather than one hundred shares that you could buy for cash) and your broker lends you $2,500.

As a lender, the broker charges you interest on the money he advances to you. Customarily, this is whatever the going bank rate is, plus a couple of percentage points for himself. How many percentage points he tacks on depends on how good business is at the time and on how good your credit rating is. Money is dearer to the poor.

The broker, you'll find, is very sensitive to the interest rate. He will emphasize it when you sign the agreement opening your margin account.

This is for two reasons: First, interest charges constitute a good piece of revenue for him; and second, quite likely he borrows the money that he lends to you. He usually borrows at something near the prime rate, or at some figure between the *prime rate* (paid by a bank's most favored customers) and the *commercial rate* (paid by consumer credit customers such as yourself). This, plus his own interest rate, is passed along to you.

Even with the broker's added interest charge the amount of interest you pay will probably be less than the rate you would pay if you, as an ordinary citizen, borrowed the money from your own bank.

When a broker borrows money from his bank, however, he doesn't want to exhaust his own line of credit, so he collateralizes the loan from the bank with the same stock that you have bought on margin. You have bought two hundred shares of stock worth five thousand dollars at current market price, so it is ample security for a loan of $2,500.

Part of the margin agreement is that you leave your stocks with the broker so that he may *hypothecate* them by pledging them to the bank as security for your loan, or for some other customer's loan if the need arises.

You will have to pay also for the commission and taxes involved in your transaction (the stock transfer tax, for instance).

You, as an investor with a private portfolio, may want to consider a feature of margin trading that rarely attracts the speculative trader who is out for big game. Even though the bank may have hypothecative control of your stock, *you* are entitled to the dividends paid on it, and if the stock has a high dividend rate, it may pay you to hold it for some time just to collect the dividends.

If your stock is paying, say, nine percent and your total interest charges are six percent, you stand to make a little extra profit just on your dividends since, buying on margin you have twice as much stock as you would have if you bought for cash.

However, most of the time a person buys a margin because he anticipates a rise in the price of the stock. That is why speculators love margin in a rising market and utilize it to escalate their profits. Real speculators don't deal in small amounts, so their profits are much larger.

If a real speculator spots the same stock you do, he is more likely to buy two thousand shares to your two hundred. He'll put up the same fifty percent margin, which comes to twenty-five thousand dollars.

Then, let's suppose that the stock rises five points and is now worth thirty dollars.

You, in your deal, would have put up $2,500 to buy two hundred shares at twenty-five dollars, and you sell two hundred shares at thirty dollars, giving you a gross profit of $3,500, less commissions, taxes and interest, but plus dividends.

The speculator on the other hand would have put up twenty-five thousand dollars to buy two thousand shares at twenty-five dollars, and he sells them at thirty dollars, or sixty thousand dollars, giving him a gross profit of thirty-five thousand dollars.

It is profits like these that make people ignore the comparatively small gains to be made by dividends, particularly dividends in relation to interest.

To get back to you and your small portfolio, however, let's suppose that the stock you bought at twenty-five dollars has now advanced to thirty dollars. While you'd like to get out of debt and clear up your margin account, you have reason to believe that the stock is destined to go still higher.

You might elect to do the conservative thing and sell eighty-one shares and pay off your margin debt of $2,500, leaving you full ownership of 119 shares, now worth a total of $3570—a profit to you on paper of over one thousand dollars.

On the other hand, you might wish to sell off your two hundred shares at thirty dollars, yielding you six thousand dollars, pay off your debt of $2,500, leaving you $3,500 in cash, which, if margin requirements are fifty percent, permits you to buy seven thousand dollars worth of another stock you think is due for a rise.

This is *playing the market*, however, and while it is perfectly normal and legal, it is the preserve of the experts. Unless you fancy yourself quite knowledgable in the ways of the stock market, it's not wise to use margin as a steady diet, but rather as something to employ on special occasions and special situations where you are sure of yourself.

For the truth is that the market can go down as well as up— and it has been known to do that.

When it does, a broker may call on you for more margin. You'll have to increase the down payment or forfeit your stock to satisfy the demand. The broker has the right to sell your stock—as much as may be necessary—to raise the money needed to cover your increased debt. And remember, brokers sell only in *round lots*, that is, one hundred shares at a time. If you have only two hundred shares, you can lose half of them on a broker's call, if you haven't the cash to put up, or you may not want to pay the call on the theory that it's unwise to send good money after bad.

The function of covering margin is not governed by the Federal Reserve Board. It is a requirement of the New York Stock Exchange and is enforceable by each broker. The Federal Reserve doesn't interfere once you have made your margined purchase. If, for instance, you bought your stock when there was a fifty percent margin requirement, the Fed would not interfere with you, even if the margin requirement was increased to one hundred percent the day after your transaction was completed. You could go your merry way with a fifty percent margin.

The Stock Exchange has a rule, though, that makes it mandatory for a broker to call on a customer for more margin whenever the amount that the customer will have in his account after selling his stocks and paying off the broker's loan adds up to less than twenty-five percent of the *current* value of the stocks.

Let's take the twenty-five dollar stock of which you own two hundred shares and for which you have borrowed $2,500 from your broker on your margin deal. If the stock falls anywhere between twenty-four dollars and sixteen dollars you are safe. But if it falls to fifteen dollars, you will get a margin call for $150. Here's why. At fifteen dollars a share your two hundred shares are worth three thousand dollars. You owe your broker $2,500, leaving you a balance of five hundred dollars. However, twenty-five percent of the current market price of three thousand dollars is $750, so the rule would be invoked, and you have to put up at least the additional $150 to cover your margin. Customarily the broker calls for more just to be safe, in the event of a further decline.

If you have reason to expect that the stock will turn around and go back to where you hoped it would be, it's worthwhile to make the extra payments.

If, however, you discover that your judgment has been wrong, it's wisest to get out of the stock and take your losses, long before it gets to a point that warrants a call for more margin.

As a rule of thumb, if the margin requirement is fifty percent, your stock can decline by one-third before a broker calls for more margin, and it can drop by two-thirds or more before a margin call if the reserve requirement is seventy-five percent.

Pyramiding your paper profits is perfectly legal today, just as it was in the dream-world of the 1920's, but with today's high margin requirements, not as many traders find it as worthwhile an exercise as they did in those halcyon times. Let's look at some comparative examples.

If you had bought your two hundred shares of twenty-five dollar stock back in the '20's', you would have had to put up only twenty percent on margin — possibly less if you were an old and valued customer of the brokerage firm. This meant that you'd have to pay one thousand dollars as down payment (twenty percent of five thousand dollars) and would own four thousands worth of stock on margin.

If your twenty-five dollar stock then went to, let's say, forty dollars, you might elect to sell your two hundred shares, which would yield you eight thousand dollars. You could then pay off your margin loan of one thousand dollars and with the seven thousand dollars remaining, you could then buy thirty-five thousand dollars worth of stock (since seven thousand dollars is twenty percent of thirty-five thousand dollars) and you would be well on your way.

In this manner, thousands of people pyramided their holdings into many millions of dollars.

The trouble came when the market began to plunge and brokers issued margin calls, only to find that their ultra-rich customers could put up only a few thousand dollars in cash on calls requiring tens of thousands. This forced them to sell the margined stocks and dump hundreds of thousands of shares into a glutted market that was already unable to absorb its sell orders, forcing prices to drop through the bottom.

If you tried the same exercise with fifty percent margin, here's how it would work out:

You'd buy two hundred shares of twenty-five dollar stock for five thousand dollars on which you'd have to put up $2,500. If the stock then jumped to forty dollars over a period of time and you decided to sell, you'd receive eight thousand dollars. You'd pay your broker's loan of $2,500, leaving you $5,500 in cash. This $5,500 would then entitle you to buy eleven thousand dollars worth of stock on a fifty percent margin.

Not nearly so profitable.

Today pyramiding is still the fastest way to build up the value of a portfolio. Aside from the technical handicap of high margin requirements, however, it must be remembered that stock prices do not often shoot up as rapidly and as consistently as they did in the days before there were so many restraints.

In even the best of markets a good stock is likely to gain only ten points in a year of rising markets, though, of course, there are obvious exceptions to this rule, even in a declining market.

So, while pyramiding through use of a margin account is plausible, it is not for the amateur or the unsure, but for the well-advised and sophisticated trader. Make sure you qualify before you try it. But that's why you're reading this book, isn't it?

XV *Hedge Your Bets: Puts and Calls*

Sooner or later the mysterious world of *puts and calls* will beckon the serious investor who reaches a point at which he wishes to protect his position or maintain his *status quo* during a period of transition, either in the market or in his own portfolio.

He will utilize these exterior devices (they're not really a regular part of the market function) either when the market is fluctuating disturbingly or when he wishes to stall for time to appraise some situation, perhaps an additional stock he wishes to buy with profit from the sale of stock currently in his portfolio.

Puts and calls are in existence to help the investor insure himself against loss and to protect a profit he has earned on paper.

If he buys a *put*, he buys the right to sell one hundred shares of a particular stock within a specific period of time at a specific price which is named in the contract.

If he buys a *call* he acquires the right to buy one hundred shares of a particular stock at a price set in the contract, within a certain period of time.

Puts and calls are accepted only on stocks listed on the New York Stock Exchange, and while executed through your broker, are traded only by a couple of dozen firms that specialize in such transactions.

They provide a useful and handy safeguard for those who know how to use them, and their functions should be considered seriously by every portfolio-building investor, for you never know when the need will arise to buy either a put or a call.

The special charm of puts and calls is that the trader himself keeps control of the situation all the way. He doesn't have to exercise either a put or a call contract if he doesn't want to. For this reason, both puts and calls are referred to as *options*.

When an investor buys a call on a stock, there is no legal obligation to exercise that option. If the price of the stock climbs, however, beyond the figure named in his contract, at any time during the period covered, he can realize a profit by "calling" on the dealer to sell him the stock at a lower price than market—the price specified in the contract.

If he buys a call and the stock drops in price, the trader obviously doesn't exercise his option, but he loses whatever he has had to pay for his call, as there is obviously no advantage in buying stock that is selling higher than the current market.

It is exactly the opposite with puts. If he buys a put, and instead of increasing in price the stock drops in price to a point lower than the figure specified in the contract, the trader can exercise his option and the dealer is obliged to buy his hundred shares at the higher price named in the contract. If the stock rises instead, he, of course doesn't exercise his option.

It's all up to the trader. He keeps control.

Puts and calls do have time limits on them. You can buy options for a standard thirty days, or you can get special options for sixty days, ninety days and 180 days. The costs are fairly well standardized so it does little good to shop around among the puts and calls specialists.

What's the price for this kind of maneuver? It varies from time to time but not by much. On a thirty-day call, the price set in the contract is usually one-and-a-half to two points above the market at the time the contract is written, and on a thirty-day put it is customarily one-and-a-half to two points below the market at contract signing.

On a thirty-day call on a stock selling at fifty dollars, with the price at one-and-one-half points to two points above market, your break-even point would be 51½ or 52. On a thirty-day put on a stock selling at 50, with the cost being one-and-one-half to two points, your break-even point would be 48½ or 48. These are not exact figures. In addition is the cash cost of 1⅜ points or $137.50 on a hundred-share deal (puts and calls are never contracted in odd-lots unless it is an unusual transaction involving extremely high-priced shares).

The cost is paid to the dealer at the signing of the contract, so it must be figured into the cost of the deal by the trader. In other words, with a call on a stock selling at 50, it must rise by more than 3⅜ points before it will pay him to exercise his option. If his fifty-dollar stock goes to, say, 55 or higher, he is in an extremely good position to make a profit and it would pay him to exercise his option.

Actually if a trader holds stock worth fifty dollars a share at the time he buys a call, he can exercise his option at 52⅞ and come out even (1½ plus 1⅜ = 52⅞).

On the longer term contracts, the dealer doesn't bother with a point spread as a general rule, but instead asks for a specific payment that might range from three hundred dollars or a little less to more than seven hundred dollars. The amount of this payment or *premium* depends on the price of the stock, of course, as well as its record of stability. If the dealer believes the stock is not going to rise or fall much in price during the term of the contract, he will quote a very favorable premium. Since he guarantees to sell you stock on a call or buy it from you on a put at specific prices, the premium for his pledge is based on how strongly he believes you will exercise your options.

It becomes apparent, then, that if you pay five hundred dollars for a ninety-day call on a hundred shares of stock selling at 50, it has to rise to rise to more than 55 before you can realize a profit within that three-month period. The opposite is true, of course, with puts. You have to be strongly convinced that your stock will post a five-point gain within three months (or a five-point loss within the same period) to make either a put or a call worth your bother.

Because the market has a generally rising trend these days, dealers are likely to charge more for a call than for a put if you buy a long-term contract, since over the long haul, the market is likely to move upward anyway. If you are contracting in a period when the market is in a long decline (and beware of sudden turn-arounds) you may find that puts are costlier.

If there can be a rule of thumb, then, it is to *trade puts and calls against the market trend,* though actually you are not buying the market, you are trading for a specific stock and you are lucky if it is countering the market—that is, one that is likely to go down when the general trend is up, or vice versa.

If a trader is trying to protect a rather costly prize, for example, shares of a stock that has recently gained a substantial number of points and promises to move still higher, he may wish to put both a put and a call on the same stock. This gives him a double vantage point from which to exercise an option if the stock takes a pronounced turn in either direction. In effect, he is protecting his position.

The puts and calls dealer has two terms for these operations. One is called a *straddle,* the other is called a *spread.*

In a straddle, both the put and call contracts are written on the basis of the current market price, so that for a fee the speculator, in effect, guarantees that he will be able to get the current price for his stock during the period of the contract regardless of whether it goes up or down. Remember, the dealer does not take points in addition to the fee on longer contracts.

In a spread, which costs less, he can buy a call a point or two above the current price and a put at a point or two below the present market in his stock.

These devices, the straddle and the spread, are useful to the speculator who expects a sudden movement in his stock, but doesn't really know in which direction.

In an unsteady market it is not unusual for a stock to spurt upwards a few points and then drop back to a new trading level.

In such an event, with the stock rising in price, the trader may make a profit by exercising the option on his call, and then, when the price of the stock drops, make another profit by opting to exercise his put.

Here's how that would work:

Suppose you bought a stock at, let's say, 40, and it has gained ten points over the past six months and is now selling at 50. You think this is about as far as it will go, but you're not sure. If the rise in price has run out of steam there might be an uneven swing in the stock for awhile, with price run-ups and then sell-offs. You like your profit of ten points (from 40 to 50) on paper, but you reason that with the expected swinging condition in the price you may be able to make a little more profit with a put and a call, so you buy a straddle.

The stock now climbs up to 55 points, so you exercise your call, making a gross profit of five points because you're buying 100 additional shares of the stock for fifty dollars a share when it's actually worth fifty-five dollars. You sell this stock in the market for fifty-five dollars a share, a gross profit of five hundred dollars on your hundred shares.

Now the stock sells off sharply and gets down to 45. You now exercise your put and sell at fifty dollars a share the stock from your portfolio which, at market, is worth only forty-five dollars a share. Again you've realized a gross profit of five hundred dollars.

With a spread instead of a straddle, you would operate in exactly the same manner under identical circumstances, but your profit would be smaller, depending on the width of your spread—how many points above the fifty dollars your call was placed and how many below fifty dollars you made your put.

It is obvious that puts and calls are primarily devices for genuine speculators, usually those who make their living by trading in the market. Such speculators utilize to direct advantage every available tool at their disposal. Puts and calls are two of their essential tools.

But what of you, the average small-time investor who has put his savings to good and profitable use by building up a modest portfolio?

Aside from the spreads and straddles, which in themselves are good protective devices, the average investor who has gained a good profit in a stock in his portfolio can safeguard it for a specific period by purchasing a put. Then if the stock falls in price, he can exercise his option and get the price that prevailed before the drop.

If he is a short-seller, of course, he can buy a call to hedge his short sale against a rise in the price of the stock that he thought was going to decline.

You may logically ask why the average investor can't better protect his stock by placing a stop loss order to sell or a stop order to buy, neither of which costs him any money, except for commissions upon execution of the order.

There is certainly nothing wrong with the stop-order technique, except that it is rigid. You have to name the price at which you wish to sell or buy, and don't forget that up-tick provision, which can be somewhat expensive.

If a man bought one hundred shares of stock at forty dollars a share and it is currently selling for fifty dollars a share, he can buy a put at the current market price for sixty days for something like two hundred dollars. Then if the stock drops, no matter how much, he can sell his put at fifty dollars a share at any time during the sixty-day period.

On the other hand, if he places a stop loss order on the same stock, he will have to pick the exact price at which he will be willing to sell, customarily a couple of points below current market. At that point he will be sold out automatically. He does not have the choice that he does with a put, where he can exercise his option as he sees fit.

Since it would cost him two hundred dollars for his put or two points (equal to one hundred dollars per point) for his stop loss order, it appears on the surface that he will come out the same with either plan.

If he places a stop loss order at 48, two points below current market, he would lose two hundred dollars on his hundred shares when his order was automatically carried out.

If he buys a put at 50, it costs him about two hundred dollars for the contract.

But suppose the stock drops by several points, then turns around a few days later and is selling at a considerably higher price than 50?

If he has had a stop loss order, he has been sold out and is out of the game.

If he has a put and hasn't exercised his option, he still owns his stock. Yet he has been protected while it has fluctuated.

Another protective technique works like this: He may sell his stock at 50 and buy a six-month call at 50 for something like $250 or perhaps a bit more (depending on the stock). If the stock drops, all he can lose is the cost of the call, but if it continues to rise, he will be in the same happy position as if he owned the stock, and, indeed, he *can* own it by exercising his option on the call. His total cost for the maneuver is the price of the call. If the call has cost him 2½ points, any gain in the stock's price of more than 52½ represents profit to him.

Another ploy is to buy a call at 50 for a six-month period, and back it up with a stop loss order at, say, 48.

Buying puts and calls costs more than trading on margin or short-selling, but it doesn't tie up the trader's money. In a fluctuating market, puts and calls may be more profitable and valuable tools than any others that are available. They are, however, for the more-than-casual and sophisticated trader who can weigh one advantage against another at any given time in the market's history—or for the skilled speculator, and frankly there aren't too many of those around, anymore. Mr. "Bet-a-Million" Gates is dead, and he left few inheritors of his skills.

You don't buy your puts and calls on the stock exchange. Although only those stocks listed on the New York Stock Exchange may be traded in puts and calls, you arrange for your put or call through your regular broker who does the transacting with the put-and-call specialist. This costs you nothing; the put-and-call dealer compensates your broker for his work. Then, if you exercise an option, either to buy or to sell, your broker gets his regular commission.

The put-and-call dealer is himself sort of a middle man. If he writes a call for you, he usually contacts someone else who, for a fee he pays, guarantees delivery of the stock to you at your price any time within the period decreed in the contract. He sells this other party the contract at a lower price than you paid for it, thereby earning his commission.

The second owner of your contract may be some very wealthy individual, but more likely it will be a big institutional investor with a huge portfolio crammed with a wide variety of stocks. It can be a trust fund, a pension fund, a foundation, a mutual fund or an insurance company. These institutionals find that they can earn a good short-term profit on their money without running much risk by buying the put-and-call dealers' contracts at discount.

In the long run, with a broad spectrum of trading, they realize a good return on their capital, while providing good accessible shelter for your short-term trades.

XVI   *Most Eggs in One Basket, Or, Dollar·Cost·Averaging*

Is there a way to play it safe and still beat the market? The experts think there may be. It's called *dollar-cost-averaging*, and it's what you do when you buy stocks on the so-called Monthly Investment Plan (so much down and a certain amount each month), and, modified, it's what you do when you buy mutual funds on the monthly payment plan.

If you have thoroughly researched a company and know for certain that its stock is worthy of your investment, you may apply the dollar-cost-averaging technique yourself, putting the same fixed amount of money into the same stock at regular intervals (monthly, quarterly, semi-annually or annually) over an extended period of time, regardless of the movement in the price of the stock.

It's not a foolproof system, of course, but it seems to work quite often.

Part of it is psychological, for with dollar-cost-averaging you are predisposed to be pleased when the stock market goes down.

For example, if you are buying one hundred dollars worth of stock each month that is currently selling at ten dollars, you will get ten shares this month, but if it drops to a market price of eight dollars a share next month, you will be able to buy not ten shares but 13 for $104. Conversely, if it increases in price to twelve dollars, you'll be able to buy only nine shares.

If you're doing your own dollar-cost-averaging, you'll have to supply the extra dollars to round out a share, such as nine shares of stock at twelve dollars will cost you $108. You will have to put up the additional eight dollars that month. If you're buying stock on the Monthly Investment Plan, your broker will buy as many shares as he can for your hundred dollar monthly payment (less commission) and will "credit" your account with the fractional shares, at the current market price.

Louis Engel, of the firm of Merrill, Lynch, Pierce, Fenner & Smith, the nation's largest brokerage firm, in his well-done book, *How To Buy Stocks* (Little, Brown and Company, Inc., 1953) stated:

"Following a system of investing a fixed sum of money in the same stock at regular intervals, you could have made a profit on probably 90 percent of the stocks listed on the New York Stock Exchange over almost any period of fifteen or twenty years you might want to pick."

This is because you would have taken advantage of two factors: you would have benefited from the general long-range trend of the market to move higher (from inflationary forces, among others) and you would have *increased* the number of shares you purchased whenever the stock fell in price.

Acting automatically this way, you would have observed one of the most basic and the soundest rules for prudent and successful investing—provided, of course, the stock that you picked was a good one.

Dollar-cost-averaging is a perfect device for those on regular income—persons with salaries or wages. Essentially it works effectively because you buy more shares of a company's stock with your fixed amount, invested at regular intervals, when the stock is low in price. Thus, when the price rises again, you make a greater profit on the larger number of shares you got at a lower price.

Because of this, your profits are realized at a surprising rate in what might be considered the normal ebb and flow of stock prices.

Let's suppose that you are able to put aside one hundred dollars a month for investment. It is difficult and costly to invest such a small amount, so you decide that you will save the hundred dollars each month and invest three hundred dollars on the first market day of each quarter.

Let us further suppose that you like a stock that has a price of ten dollars when you are first attracted to it and begin to buy it. Then, over the ensuing months your stock drops point by point to five dollars, turns around and climbs point by point to fifteen dollars, and then turns around again and drops point by point to the ten dollar price it started with. If you sell out at that point, you will realize a greater profit than you might imagine, solely because of those lower-cost shares in your portfolio.

Here's how it works:

Price Per Share	Number of Shares Bought	Total Cost of Shares	Number of Shares Now Owned	Accumulating Cost of Shares	Total Value of Shares
$10	30	$300	30	$ 300	$ 300
9	34	306	64	606	576
8	39	304	103	910	824
7	44	308	147	1218	1109
6	50	300	197	1518	1182
5	60	300	257	1818	1285
6	50	300	307	2118	1842
7	44	308	351	2426	2457
8	39	304	390	2816	3120
9	34	306	424	3122	3816
10	30	300	454	3422	4540
11	28	308	482	3730	5302
12	25	300	507	4030	6084
13	24	312	531	4392	6903
14	22	308	553	4700	7742
15	20	300	573	5000	8595
14	22	308	595	5308	8330
13	24	312	619	5620	8047
12	25	300	644	5920	7728
11	28	308	672	6228	7392
10	30	300	702	6528	7020

Now, of course, no stock fluctuates with such magnificent precision from ten dollars down to five dollars, then back up to ten dollars and on up to fifteen dollars, and down to ten dollars. A stock may well swing in a range between five, ten and fifteen dollars, but it is unlikely to record such rhythmic sequential changes. For the purpose of illustrating the efficacy of dollar-cost-averaging, however, you must imagine that you have purchased a stock that behaves in such an orderly manner in the marketplace.

It has taken you 21 quarters—five years and one month—to reach the point where you own 702 shares of this stock.

You have paid $6,528 for them, and they are worth, at the current ten dollar market price, $7,020. You show a profit here of $492, or seven percent. Not bad.

However, let's assume that this company pays an eighty-cent annual dividend, payable at the rate of twenty cents per share quarterly. We will assume also that, being smart in the ways of the market, you purchase your shares each quarter in time to get in on the *record date;* that is, in time to collect the dividend.

Thus, on the basis of twenty cents per share on the number of shares owned each quarter, you would have received in dividends a total of $1,720.40. This, added to your market value profit of $492, gives you a total gain of $2,212—or thirty-seven percent of your investment!

And you still own your stocks.

It can be seen from the table of figures that the widest spread of profit between the amount of money invested and the market value of the stocks was when it reached fifteen dollars a share in the market. If you had sold then, your total investment in 573 shares of stock would have been five thousand dollars, and you would have realized a profit of $3,595. At that time you would have collected $1,074 in dividends. This means that your profit would have been $4,669 ($3,595 plus $1,074)—almost double your investment of $5,000.

That would have been the time to sell, of course, or to have placed a stop loss order at fourteen dollars. Or, you might have bought a straddle at fifteen dollars.

For the purpose of this exercise, however, we continued to buy the stock each quarter in the expectation that even if it does go back to ten dollars, there's a good chance that ultimately it will climb back to fifteen dollars again.

The table will reveal that you are actually fortunate if your stock drops off in price after you have started on a quarterly purchase plan of your own, simply because it permits you to acquire more shares for your money. You keep buying in confidence that the market will recover, as it always has, and that when it reaches ten dollars again, you will be much better off than if it had stayed at ten dollars all along.

At the recovery point of ten dollars on the table, you'll see that you own 454 shares of stock for which you have paid only $3,422 with a market value of $4,540, a profit of $1,118, or about thirty-three percent on your investment.

If the stock had remained constant at ten dollars through each quarter for those same eleven quarters when, in our table it dropped to five dollars and then recovered to ten dollars, here's how it would have worked out for you (at three hundred dollars invested per quarter):

Price Per Share	Number of Shares Bought	Total Cost of Shares	Number of Shares Now Owned	Accumulating Cost of Shares	Total Value of Shares
$10	30	$300	30	$ 300	$ 300
10	30	300	60	600	600
10	30	300	90	900	900
10	30	300	120	1200	1200
10	30	300	150	1500	1500
10	30	300	180	1800	1800
10	30	300	210	2100	2100
10	30	300	240	2400	2400
10	30	300	270	2700	2700
10	30	300	300	3000	3000
10	30	300	330	3300	3300

You would have paid $3,300 for stock that was worth, at market value, precisely the same—$3,300.

You would own 330 shares of the stock worth ten dollars a share instead of the 454 you would own if the market had dropped off.

This is the heart of dollar-cost-averaging. It anticipates fluctuations in the market and, hopefully, soon after you begin the program. This is called *averaging down* and it is a handier device than you might think after only superficial consideration.

How many times have you heard someone say, "The market is too high right now," as the reason for not buying securities at that time. What this person is really saying is that he thinks prices are going to drop in the near future.

If he really believes this, then it is time to embark on a program of dollar-cost-averaging—to make regular purchases—in order to capitalize on this phenomenon.

In the long run, the market always increases in value. Pick almost any extended period in market history and you will see that prices of securities rise, sometimes rapidly, sometimes slowly, sometimes with broad fluctuations. This was true even during the great depression of the 1930's when prices recovered from the 1929 crash.

The major requirements of a dollar-cost-averaging program are, in order, the three Big C's—Cash, Courage and Constancy.

You need Cash to make it work. You need Courage to keep buying your stock in the face of falling prices, in order to build up the number of shares in your portfolio. You need to maintain your program Constantly, and on a regular basis.

It takes courage to keep buying in the face of a falling market. And it must be remembered that when the market is selling off, business conditions may also be softening, and your own income may be affected, making it harder to maintain your plan of purchases.

If the amount you have available to invest comes to the exact penny each month or each quarter, you won't be able to buy your stocks "to the nearest share", as you did in the table. Then you spent more than three hundred dollars on several occasions, one time going as high as $312.

If all you are going to have available is three hundred dollars each quarter—three hundred dollars and nothing more—you should consider joining a Monthly Investment Plan which will be made available to you by your broker.

Under this program you sign a contract to buy three hundred dollars worth of a specific stock each quarter. The broker sells it to you in shares and fractional shares, carried out to the fourth decimal point, so that you get exactly three hundred dollars worth of stock for your money. In fact, the sum invested is minus brokerage commissions and the ⅛th point commission due to the odd-lot dealer (for you're buying in odd lots, that is, less than one hundred shares).

The broker and odd-lot dealer buy your stock at the opening market price on the day following receipt of your quarterly payment.

You may buy on a monthly plan or a quarterly plan and receive the same fractional-share deal with your broker.

Your contract may be cancelled at any time, without penalty, and, indeed, if you wish to skip a couple of installments, you may do so without loss of contract or any other kind of penalty.

The Monthly Investment Plan is Wall Street's attempt to get into the mass-marketing business. It is actually a conventional pay-as-you-go installment plan, geared to the everyday wage-earner with a predictable income and savings program.

It offers the person who lacks the capital required to get into the market a chance to become an investor on a regular basis.

If you are constant in your Monthly (or Quarterly) Investment Plan you can garner the same effect as you can by dollar-cost-averaging.

You can cancel your contract and sell your shares at any time you wish. The broker will sell as many whole shares as you own, and will give you cash credit for the fractional shares remaining in your account.

When you accumulate 50 shares of stock in your M.I.P. program, you will receive a certificate. You may also order a certificate for fewer shares, for a token fee.

XVII *Rights and*
Warrants Beckon

A good way to avoid extra profits in the stock market is to remain in ignorance of the function of *rights* and *warrants*. As an exercise in testing the widespread disregard for these by-products of corporate growth, the author visited two Wall Street boardrooms one morning and talked with half a dozen people in each one about some warrants that were at the time quite popular among the professional traders. Only two of the people in one boardroom and only one in the other knew anything at all about how warrants come into existence, how they are traded, and of what value they are to the investor.

The nine who knew nothing about rights and warrants were people with money invested in the market, sophisticated enough to be watching the printout of symbols and figures on the electronic tape. They were *watching* the phenomenon of the auction market and in some measure they were participating in it, but it was apparent that they didn't fully understand it.

Rights or warrants are quite often the by-product of corporate expansion and are issued when a company needs to raise money, preferably from existing stockholders, for new plants or equipment. Since this usually promises to yield higher income to the company and higher dividends to those who own stock, the rights or warrants are frequently in demand by traders who are alert to their appearance on the market.

Rights are the same as warrants and *vice versa*. When you own them, they are called rights. When you're selling them, they're called warrants. Actually, no matter what you call them, they are certificates that entitle the holder to buy the stock of a corporation at a specific price (usually below current market price) on or before a specific date. In a manner of speaking, they are options to buy. Unlike options, however, they may be traded openly among buyers and sellers, so they are called rights to buy.

Let's consider the case of Lymphatic Lamp Company, formed half a dozen years ago in the small town of Incandescence, Pennsylvania, where an entrepreneur induced twenty local businessmen to put up one thousand dollars each, for which each received a hundred shares of stock worth ten dollars per share, to capitalize the company for twenty thousand dollars.

Lymphatic Lamp has grown and prospered in the six years since it was started, producing good electrical fixtures for home and office, barber shop and beauty parlor, and the company has not only paid dividends each year at the rate of one dollar annually or ten per cent of the original price of the stock, but it has been able to build a bank account of retained earnings (that is, earnings that are not paid out as dividends and are not plowed back into the business to meet operating costs) so that now the company is capitalized at forty thousand dollars, exactly twice what it was when it commenced operations.

That means, in effect, that the stock of the original investors is worth twenty dollars a share. That's a theoretical figure because Lymphatic Lamp would have to be liquidated in order to realize a return of twenty dollars a share, and nobody wants to do that.

Indeed, the board of directors of Lymphatic Lamp is making plans to expand its operations to meet a rising market for electrical fixtures. It wants an additional forty thousand dollars in cash to accomplish its goals.

With twenty thousand dollars in the bank and twenty thousand dollars in capital goods (plant and equipment) the directors should have no trouble borrowing forty thousand dollars from the banks. It's the kind of situation the Small Business Administration would be glad to underwrite through one of its programs.

But with the higher costs of construction these days, the directors decided they'd need every penny of that forty thousand dollars in new money, and wouldn't like to become involved in installment payments to the banks because it would drain off needed cash.

Instead it was voted to sell stock to raise the additional capital. At the time Lymphatic Lamp was formed it authorized five thousand shares of stock, but issued only two thousand shares (one hundred shares each to twenty business leaders in Incandescence). It has three thousand remaining shares of authorized but unissued stock, so the directors voted to sell one thousand additional shares.

The price on these new shares would normally be the current market price, which at the time was twenty-four dollars per share.

But the directors liked the set-up the way it was. The existing stockholders were exceptionally pleased with their investments in Lymphatic Lamp and, as a result, were well disposed toward the management and did not interfere with operations or policy. Thus the directors wished to not broaden the ownership of Lymphatic Lamp if it could be avoided.

Therefore the board of directors decided to issue rights to all existing stockholders to buy one new share of stock at twenty dollars per share for each share of stock now owned. This meant that one hundred shares was priced at two thousand dollars at a time when the current market price was $24. If a stockholder bought one hundred shares in the open market it would cost him $2,400.

Of course, there were more than twenty stockholders now. Some of the original investors had died and their shares were distributed among members of their families. Others had decided to take the profit on their investments and had sold the stock to other investors. Some had needed cash and had sold out.

Some, however, for reasons best known to themselves, chose to sell their rights. Perhaps they needed the money. Or possibly they thought some other stock offered greater promise.

They offered their rights for sale at two dollars.

Why not four dollars? After all the market for the stock is $24.

The formula for figuring the value of rights works like this:

Prevailing Price of Stock:	$24
Minus price in warrant:	20
	$ 4
Divide by number of old shares needed to buy one new share: (plus one additional share)	
1 + 1 is 2	2
Divide this by remainder, above: $4 ÷ 2	$ 2

At the outset there were not any takers for the available rights. There was good reason for this lack of interest. The rights offered a slim bargain. At a cost of two dollars per share the warrants entitled the buyer to purchase a share of stock at twenty dollars. His total price would be twenty-two dollars per share, only two dollars under current market.

On the surface it might have *seemed* like a bargain, this spread of two dollars between the warrant price and the current market price, but it remained to be seen if Lymphatic Lamp would complete its subscription.

As soon as it was announced that most of the stockholders had exercised their rights and the subscription was nearly completed, the price of the warrants rose.

That rise in price stimulated interest in the few available warrants. As investors investigated the situation they realized that when Lymphatic Lamp was tooled up to new production it would begin to reap handsome earnings, and they began to bid up the price of the warrants and soon they were selling above par at six dollars. That meant that anyone exercising their rights would be paying twenty-six dollars a share for the Lymphatic Lamp stock.

Again, this seems like inconsistent thinking. But it isn't when you consider that the rights may be exercised at any time within one year of the issuing date of the warrant.

What it means, simply, is that the fellow who is willing to pay a six dollar premium to buy a twenty dollar stock truly believes that the market price of that stock will be greater than twenty-six dollars within the next year, and at the rate the company has been growing, it seems a good bet.

When major corporations, whose securities are listed on the New York Stock Exchange, issue warrants, the prices of those warrants are quoted by the Exchange and are listed in the newspapers.

Some corporations have issued warrants with no expiration date. These are called *perpetual warrants*. Among them are the warrants of Alleghany Corporation, Jefferson Lake Asbestos, and Tri-Continental Corporation.

It is surprising how many people ignore warrants from companies whose stock they own, neither exercising them nor selling them, but holding them in useless and worthless escrow, until they expire.

American Telephone & Telegraph Company learned that it must maintain a constant promotion effort to get all of its stockholders to do something about their warrants. Without urging from the company, thousands would allow their warrants to expire and become worthless.

Many professional advisers contend that stock warrants are fun to own—exciting—but that they are risky.

I do not believe they are any riskier than owning shares of common stock. The requirement is that the purchaser be well-informed about the warrant, and that is a basic requirement for anything you do about risking your money on an investment of any kind. The money you put into any stock transaction is called Risk Capital, and it's so named for a most valid reason.

Warrants offer a chance for large percentage gains without risking or exposing much capital. Small amounts of money can buy your admission to what might be a most profitable venture. On some warrants, such as Tri-Continental Corporation, for instance, fine fortunes were made by the faithful in the 1950's and '60's.

It takes courage to trade in most warrants because they can nosedive as rapidly as they can climb, and a chart of many of them would look like a dangerous roller coaster. For this reason they are not for the faint of heart.

What they offer is a unique way to share in the activity of the stock market without any significant outlay of cash. Several investors of the author's acquaintance make a practice of liquidating their securities whenever they think the market is too high, but maintain a finger in the pie by diverting small amounts of money into warrants. If they are actively traded, warrants can become the inexpensive "game stocks" that satisfy the investors with sporting blood.

There is always as much disagreement as there is agreement in the stock market, and if you believe that a certain stock with rights and warrants is due to increase in price, there are certain to be those who think otherwise and may want to divest themselves of their rights. They won't want to exercise a warrant to buy stock at twenty dollars when they think it's going to drop to fifteen dollars. But if you think it's going to increase to twenty-six dollars or more, you're a customer for a warrant that sells for two dollars, giving you the right to buy twenty dollar stock that's worth twenty-six dollars.

The three basic questions to ask yourself before trading in warrants are:

1. How much will it cost me to exercise the warrant and buy a share of stock through conversion?

2. Is there protection against dilution through stock splits or stock dividends?

3. What is the length of time that the warrant runs?

XVIII *Understanding the News*

There are many days when the front page of your newspaper seems totally unrelated to the financial pages. Just as often the news in the financial section seems unconnected in any fashion with the reports of prices in the stock table.

One page one may be a story of Congress enacting a new tax bill that will take a huge bite out of spendable income, which leads you to believe that surely this will mean lower profits for many corporations. But on turning to the stock tables you'll find that the market generally advanced in price.

In the financial section may be a story that retail sales generally are much higher this quarter than they were last, but a check of the stock list will show that the stocks of the big retailers sold lower.

Steel profits are up, but the prices of steel stocks are down.

How come? Are traders being contrary, or are they slow to react to news? Will their reaction come a day later?

These amazing paradoxes occur almost daily and to the uninitiated it adds to the problem of trying to understand financial news and profit from it.

For this phenomenon there is a relatively simple explanation. It's called *discounting*—not to be confused with the practice of selling something at a reduced price.

Contrary to the notion that the stock market is slow to react to situations, more often than not it *anticipates* them and *discounts* them in advance.

The well-informed traders in Wall Street knew, for instance, that Congress would pass the bill raising taxes, its probable effects had been analyzed and appropriate investment moves had been made weeks in advance. Had Congress failed to enact the legislation, the market might have reacted violently.

The same holds true for the rise in retail profits, for the increase in steel earnings, and for almost any news that is in any way predictable.

Thus your newspaper is not what it appears to be. The news in the stock tables is tied to the news in the financial section and to that in the front section of the newspaper.

If you wish to hunt a bit you can find most news in the paper even more tightly meshed. A story by the science editor on a new wonder drug may not be reflected in today's stock table prices, but you can bet your last dollar that days, weeks or months before, traders had *discounted* the effects of the new drug and had anticipated improved profits for the manufacturers of it and others involved with it. But again this boils down to the individual companies; a firm with a huge debt or manned by an inept management may have a marvelous new product, but remain an unlikely candidate for big profits.

If the economy may be described as a dog, the stock market is the tail of this economic canine, and it is a barometric tail. It is not a tail that wags the dog, but it is a tail that, in being wagged, reveals the health and spirit of the dog.

It is an anticipatory tail. It watches closely, and if the dog eats some wholesome food, it signals good health even before the nutrients have had a chance to go to work. And *vice versa.*

In a way, this extends the art of contrary thinking into a broad area because the sharp traders are, in effect, doing what is not expected of them.

Many people, including some learned economists, believe that the stock market is an infallible barometer that signals upcoming trends in general business. Much of the time this is true, but it is unwise to count on the market to be accurately barometric. The stock market is too selective these days, and too many companies are broadly diversified, with profits coming from a wide range of separate sources, to provide an unassailable forecast.

Let's say it's about as good at economic forecasting as meteorological instruments are at predicting the weather. How many times has the forecaster expected "light, scattered showers," when instead you were deluged with an unscheduled downpour? Roughly speaking, that's about how accurate the stock market is at predicting how the general economy will fare in the months ahead.

The average investor should read thoroughly the financial news that accompanies the stock tables in his newspaper. If it's skimpy, as so many financial sections are these days, he should subscribe to a good daily newspaper that carries such news. Without it, he is trading blindly. It is news that can be mined for the information that leads to profits on his investments.

The *Wall Street Journal* exists, thrives and grows because of the failure of newspapers of general circulation to cover the business and financial world with any depth or discernment. This is strange when you think that newspapers, a majority of which enjoy monopoly markets, are regarded by most owners as supporters, if not defenders, of the private enterprise system. Many treat capitalism as if they had invented it personally and in their editorial columns show an almost paternal attitude toward it. It is a viewpoint that is not often carried through to the financial sections of their newspapers, however, where space limitations and unimaginative editing result in news fare that is of questionable value to investor-readers.

An announcement that Joe Jones of 814 Central Avenue has been promoted to head local sales for the Iceberg Freezer and Refrigerator Company *is* news and it *is* important to the folks in Joe's hometown, but it is of no value to a person who owns stock in Iceberg Freezer and Refrigerator Company.

It is very doubtful that the local paper will carry an announcement of the election of the new president and chief executive officer of Iceberg Freezer and Refrigerator because the home office is located far away, in Chicago, and it's not local news. Yet that news *is* of importance to the investor, because the calibre of the man heading the operation is vital to future earnings.

Many newspapers carry only partial listings in their stock tables, as though it could be determined by someone on the paper just what securities would be owned locally. I have even seen lists that were chopped off in the middle so that the paper printed quotations of stocks whose names begin with "A" through "M" only. Imagine the reaction from the front office if the television schedule should be cut off at the noon listing?

In a newspaper with a well-rounded and professionally edited financial section you will find a welter of important information about general business, about the government, about industrial trends and activities, and about individual companies, all of which bear on your investments.

Some of the stories may seem a trifle too optimistic. This is because they are furnished by the companies themselves and prepared by their public relations representatives. But there are several factors working against over-optimism. First, responsible newspapers today make a sincere effort to be objective and editors weed out a good deal of the self-aggrandizing material that crops up in the press releases. Second, the Securities and Exchange Commission monitors all such releases if they come from companies that are publicly owned, and has an elaborate set of rules governing the issuance of much information. Third, the companies, themselves, must be careful for it's easy to get a reputation as a phoney and this they try to avoid.

As an investor you should take cognizance of news of companies if you know they are publicly held, for what affects one frequently concerns several sooner or later, particularly if they are in the same market or the same industry.

Among the more important news stories of companies are:

-Expansion plans.
-Sales and earnings records.
-Merger discussions.
-Top-echelon promotions or hirings.
-New Products.
-Building programs.
-Marketing plans.
-Production records.

It is not necessary to own stock in a company to find investment information in its news stories. If you own stock in Zenith and read that RCA television set sales are falling, you had better pay attention. If you read that RCA is enjoying a rise in sales of TV sets, you'll want to find out whether Zenith is having the same experience.

The *market lead* is the big story each day in the financial section, and while it is informative in reporting what happened to various issues and segments of the list during the previous session, it is of greater value to every investor in disclosing the current trend of the market.

There was a time when the larger newspapers stationed their own experts, so-called, in Wall Street to file the daily market leader, but today, with the exception of the New York papers, the stories are filed either by Associated Press or United Press International.

The *New York Times* and the *Wall Street Journal* carry their own market stories and generally they are loaded with nuggets of valuable information for almost every investor, no matter how small his holdings. The wire service market leads are also written by professionals who do a good job under tough deadlines, so it behooves the investor to read what they file.

From these stories you'll get a good idea of what the professional traders are thinking and doing, and it should guide you in making your own plans. If the market story says that the *selling* "met resistance," you'll know that the professionals rallied around and began to buy stocks. If *buying* meets with "resistance," but it doesn't drop prices by much, you'll know that the traders believe the levels are just about right.

There is a jargon that is used, and newcomers to the marketplace often criticize it, but it is as essential in describing accurately what happened as is the patois of sports writers in pursuing their craft. Don't worry about the Wall Street terms. You'll catch on quickly, and if you don't, just ask your broker exactly what is meant by a word or a phrase that puzzles you. He'll be glad to help. He wants you reading the financial pages, too. That's where he advertises.

The main point to remember about the stock market when relating it to general business conditions and the state of the economy is that it is virtually unreliable. Most importantly, it doesn't always respond as it should. When inflation is threatened, for instance, that is a sign of ill health in the economy, and one supposes that the market will register a drop in prices.

Quite the contrary, stock prices are almost certain to rise in the face of inflation, first because of buying pressure brought on by the knowledge that stocks are a good refuge for inflation, and second, because when corporate prices rise, corporate profits usually also rise, and the stocks are expected to acquire greater value.

In addition, it is self-evident that if the stock market doesn't anticipate the business trend, it must ultimately conform with it, so that its value for prognosticating purposes is neutralized.

To arm yourself with the information you need to evaluate the economy, there are certain small tables and indices that appear in the financial sections of good newspapers on regular schedules, and you should watch for them.

The most important of these, according to most investors, is the Federal Reserve Board's Index of Industrial Production. Perhaps the second most important appears Mondays, an index of steel production prepared by *Steel Magazine* and the American Iron and Steel Institute.

Others that you should be cognizant of include electrical production, housing starts, construction, railroad carloadings, industrial orders, industrial inventories, auto output, machine tool production, cotton spindlage, and farm prices.

It is not necessary to keep your own charts or even to try to remember the exact figures. You'll notice quickly enough, if machine tool orders begin to fall, or if farm prices start climbing skyward.

After you notice the simple figures in these indices, it is up to you to draw your own conclusions, make your own interpretations, and act according to your own judgment.

In my own view, I regard machine tool orders as among the more sensitive barometers for the industrial list of stocks. Machine tools are essential to companies that plan new models or new products, and the orders for them reflect rather sensitively the plans of the industrial corporations.

This was more important a quarter of a century ago (as was cotton spindlage) than is the case today when so much of the national wealth and well-being is based on a service economy. But even with the growth of the service industries machine tools still count. The man who owns a gas station, which is purely a service operation, should be concerned about whether the Detroit automobile companies are going to build and sell many cars this year.

As an investor in a petroleum company stock, so should you. You'd be concerned if you owned a rubber company stock or a chemical company stock or a steel stock or a railroad stock, for they all depend in some measure on the automobile companies, and the auto companies buy machine tools.

XIX   *Let George Do It: Clubs, Funds and Trusts*

Even for the most skilled professional there is always a temptation to enlist the aid of someone else to make your investment decisions for you. That way you always have someone to blame if something goes wrong. The effects of a bad decision are no less harmful if someone else did the decision-making, but at least you have someone to share the sorrow.

The desire to have other shoulders to weep on is one of the reasons that investment clubs were first formed. Another important reason is that by pooling the resources of several members of a club, substantial amounts of stock can be purchased, avoiding the extra cost of buying in odd lots.

Investment clubs seem to be increasingly popular, through good times and bad, through bull markets and bear. Many of them, it must be admitted, are ineffective and have become more social than practical. If they're profitable for the members, it's likely to result more from luck than wisdom and judgment. Some clubs can even be harmful if they disseminate incorrect or confusing information.

Some, however, are excellent. They make money for their members, and their sessions are both interesting and educational.

In the absence of any official studies on the subject of investment clubs, I undertook my own research to find out how the better-functioning ones are organized.

Most of the clubs thus reviewed were found to be in four broad categories:

-Clubs formed by groups of neighbors.

-Clubs formed in business offices.

-Clubs formed within other organizations—fraternal, social or patriotic.

-Clubs formed among people who have common interests (business, professional, sports, hobbies, etc.).

They usually start informally when a small group of people begin discussing the stock market or their own investments. The origins of many clubs go back to some wistfully expressed wish, such as, "If only I had more money to invest I'd be buying Palmetto Fan stock right now . . ."

Sooner or later someone gets the bright idea that if everyone in the group invested a little amount there would result a sufficient sum to purchase a significant block of Palmetto Fan.

The investment club, then, is a loose organization designed to accommodate the pooling of members' contributions so they can invest in equal shares of a specific stock.

Conventionally the clubs appoint a Treasurer, who looks out for the regular dues or payments of members, and a Portfolio Manager who does the buying and selling, either on instruction from a board of directors or by vote of the whole membership.

It's rare for the Portfolio Manager of an investment club to be agreeable to buying stock unless there is a vote of the full membership of the club. That way the responsibility is shared by all.

Clubs must be governed by ironclad rules. First, the members must make regular payments of specified amounts. Second, a specific vote (say, two-thirds of the membership) must be final, and dissenters must agree to go along with the majority. Otherwise the entire structure crumbles and the adventure in quest of profits becomes a family donnybrook.

Sometimes clubs are formed for a single purpose and with a single goal. These are usually hastily organized to pool resources for the purchase of one issue of stock, quite often a very expensive one. The purchase having been made, the club remains in force only until the stock is sold and the profits, if any, are divided among the members.

More popular are clubs that are formed by small groups, say ten or a dozen people, with an agreement to have each member invest a fixed amount each month, say twenty-five dollars. If there are ten members, this allows the purchase of $250 worth of some kind of stock each month.

There are many clubs that have an investment fee of one hundred dollars each month, and I encountered a couple that require each member to invest one thousand dollars each month. It must be remembered, though, that anyone who can invest a thousand dollars a month can usually afford the best professional advice available, and he also has tax problems.

Remember too that anyone who can invest forty dollars or more each month can participate in the Monthly Investment Plan as described in preceding chapters.

Many clubs try to arrange to have speakers attend some of their sessions, usually experts in one or another of the special fields of investing. There is always a question as to the value of these speakers, for real experts can rarely be induced to speak for small fees, and more often than not the speaker turns out to be a salesman from one of the brokerage houses or mutual funds.

More valuable is a speaker from an older and more established investment club who can tell you how to organize along constructive lines and can review some of the typical portfolios of *his* club. He can also review his club's mistakes.

Ideally an investment club should invest for long-term gains and should resolve at the outset not to be distracted by the peaks and valleys of market fluctuations. There should be a firm decision to buy a stock at a certain price and to sell it at a certain price, and t'hell with what happens in between.

The more successful clubs have a president who parcels out research assignments. One member might be charged with the task of scouting out investment possibilities and making recommendations of new companies and stocks to be researched.

Another might be asked to research the management of a company that is being considered for investment; a third member can be given the assignment of preparing a report on that company's products and markets; a fourth can be asked to present a study of the company's financial statement and annual report; a fifth may be asked to collect and present research articles and analyses of the company and its stock that have been prepared by experts in the brokerage houses.

In this manner, all the details about a company's operations can be presented to the full membership before it votes on whether or not to buy the stock.

Investment clubs can be useful to the beginner, provided the club is not formed entirely of beginners. In a well-organized and successful club the novice can learn how best to research and analyze a stock. At the very least he'll learn what to look for in making an appraisal of a company.

Some clubs successfully manage to combine social activities with the stern business of investments. The charges levied against members are padded by a specific amount to accommodate a special fund for refreshments or sometimes even for entertainment. Experience has shown that the serving of drinks, both the sturdy kind and soft drinks, has helped tired breadwinners through the "informational" part of a research discussion.

A good club is not too large—perhaps ten or twenty members. The amount of regular investment for each member should not be too large, in the range of twenty-five to fifty dollars per month, nor should it be too small to be effective.

Some are run like closed-end investment trusts, and once the agreed-upon membership has been reached, it is closed and no further members are accepted until a member wishes to sell out his portion of the investment portfolio.

Others operate with less formal restrictions, and after the purchase of one "phase" or one particular issue of stock, open the membership rolls for the next step in the acquisition of securities.

To understand the workings of an *investment trust* it is necessary only to take a step back from the local investment club and envision a much grander operation. It is a closed-end fund, meaning that once it has been capitalized, no further capital will be admitted, and its shares are traded at a value that is determined between buyer and seller.

To illustrate:

Let's assume that you have ten thousand dollars you wish to invest, and you just happen to know of nine other people who each have ten thousand dollars that they want to invest.

Instead of each one of you investing ten thousand dollars, you pool your money and invest one hundred thousand dollars.

Then, instead of functioning as an investment club where you will be governed by the decisions of ten people, each with an identical interest in the venture, you decide to hire an expert manager and have him invest in a good portfolio of stocks.

Your expert manager turns out to be a good one and the portfolio immediately begins to show gains. At the end of the year the hundred thousand dollars is now worth $125,000.

Each investor who put in ten thousand dollars now owns a share of a trust valued at $12,500.

If the ten investors decide to remain an investment trust, they will vote not to allow more capital to be invested but to allow any original investor to sell his portion for whatever price he can get. Since it is now worth $12,500 and has shown a twenty-five percent gain in one year, presumably an investor who wished to sell could get a very good price for his share.

If, on the other hand, it was decided to allow other investors to get into the act and take advantage of the expert manager, the investors will vote to allow anyone to join up for an investment of $12,500.

This would make it a *mutual fund.*

Both investment trusts and mutual funds have been growing in popularity since the early 1950's, though they have been in existence since the last century. Basically, they answer the need of the private investor who is too busy, too lazy or too dumb to do his own investing. They also meet one other need, by allowing a person to become an investor with a very small investment. They also permit him to benefit from very expensive and expert management.

A mutual fund is also called an open-end trust, meaning that it can keep growing in the number of participants, as opposed to the closed-end trust, which cannot.

Closed-end trusts are companies whose shares are bought and sold—traded on the market—just like other corporations. They are businesses, and their business is to invest in the capital stock of other companies. Instead of making products, they are in the business of buying stock of companies that do make products, or perform services, or explore for minerals or petroleum.

The stock of closed-end trusts is traded Over-the-Counter and shares can be bought through your regular broker for his regular commission.

More often than not you can buy a share of an investment trust (closed-end) at a price that is lower than its net asset value per share. This is no reflection on the management of the trust; it is merely that investors realize that if the trust were to be liquidated, the mere dumping of so many shares of stock on the market would depress the price, hence reduce the value of each share held.

Sometimes, however, you'll find one selling at a premium. Generally speaking, the price per share of an investment trust is in the neighborhood of its net asset value per share.

Shares of an open-end trust—a mutual fund—are always bought and sold on the basis of their *exact* net value, a figure that is computed twice each trading day. This is the price that a dealer will charge if you buy. It is also the price he will pay if you sell.

You can buy mutual fund stock outright at the stated price per share or you can buy it on a regular monthly payment plan of the kind that has brought enormous, sometimes embarrassing, growth to the mutual fund industry.

While you pay a regular brokerage commission to buy or sell an investment trust stock, you pay a *front end load* cost on many mutual funds. This cost, ranging up to eight percent and even higher, is for selling and distribution costs, and it usually provides the broker or salesman with about six percent for himself. This fact alone results in some strenuous efforts to sell mutual funds. Added to that cost is a regular charge—again a load charge—for management of the fund. This is about one-half of one percent, or slightly higher, but it amounts to a substantial sum in the long run.

Despite these drawbacks, mutual funds have become exceedingly popular with small investors. Millions own them.

The funds themselves justify the loading charges by pointing out that they are prohibited from doing any advertising to speak of. Instead, they say, they must put their entire selling effort into the man who makes the sale.

The Securities and Exchange Commission prohibits the mutual funds from advertising anything except with what the trade calls *tombstone ads*. These merely carry the name of the fund or the dealer. They cannot even state that the fund has a good record.

The reason for this is that mutual funds are constantly issuing new stock—their own. The Securities and Exchange Commission regulations state that a stock cannot be advertised until it has been in existence for a year. Before that time, it can be mentioned only in a prospectus.

A prospectus is what you get when you inquire about a particular mutual fund. After that you'll most likely get a call from a salesman. He will explain that a great deal cannot be put in writing because of the SEC's regulation. This is true, of course, but a fund *can* show you its record over the past several years, and this is something you want to study carefully.

Look particularly at the net asset value per share during the bear market of 1969–1970. See how the fund held up under the strong selling pressures of that period.

The merchandising techniques of the mutual funds—whether justified or not—offend some of the more staid and conservative members of the Wall Street community and it is likely that if you express an interest in funds you will find many people who will speak against them.

On performance, however, in general the funds have done well, and a great many Americans who otherwise would not have been stockholders have been introduced to the thrifty habits of investing. In many respects the mutual funds brought Wall Street to Main Street better than any other program that has emanated from the financial district.

The front load costs may be considered in another light. If you buy almost anything on time you pay a substantial finance charge. When you are in a monthly plan for the purchase of mutual funds, you are, in effect, buying on time and paying accordingly.

It's an expensive way to invest, just as buying a house with a mortgage is an expensive way to become a property owner, but if you haven't got the cash, it's a convenient—and necessary—way to do it.

Mutual funds offer the small investor protection that he otherwise could not provide for himself. The funds' managers usually strive for diversification, and invest broadly across the entire spectrum of securities. Thus, if the price of stocks in the steel industry is depressed, it may be countered by a rise in the price of stocks in the automotive industry.

If a man can afford to buy only one stock, as in the Monthly Investment Plan, he is obviously taking on a greater risk than he is by making an investment of the same amount each month in a mutual fund, one share of which may well represent scores of different companies.

This is not to say that the managers of mutual funds are all geniuses. The record will show that they are anything but. By Monday-morning quarterbacking, it is possible to demonstrate that in almost any year the managers, in general, could have done much better than they did. However, it is easy to determine at the year's end that ABC Corporation, which you didn't buy, advanced in price twice as much as XYZ Corporation, which you did.

There are certain things you should do before you buy *any* mutual fund.

1. *Shop around.* There are now several hundred open-ended funds available to you. You don't have to settle for the one you have heard about or the one whose salesman has called on you.

2. *Check the record.* Insist that you look at the performance sheet for several years past. Check them against other funds' records.

3. *Check the operating statement.* How much money has the fund borrowed? Some are severely in debt, and even if they are investing successfully, if they're doing it on borrowed money, it is of small benefit to you.

4. *Check the load factor.* What percentage of your purchase price goes for load? This figure now varies widely, and you should get the best deal you can.

5. *Check the management fees.* These, too, vary widely, and you can pay from fractions of one percent up to a full percentage point.

6. *Check the redemption fee.* Some funds penalize you for selling out your shares before a certain date. The redemption fee should be small and it should compare favorably with other funds of similar size.

7. *Check the terms of your contract or agreement.* Many funds today make you agree to purchase shares over a certain period of time with payments to be made on a certain schedule. The contracts or agreements frequently call for expensive penalties if you do not send in your money on time. Don't buy a fund that is making its money this way—it's obvious that it's not able to do well in the market.

XX How to Keep
Your Broker Honest

No kid really wants to be a thief, but every parent knows that he may become one if you leave him alone in an unattended candy store. And if you leave the keys in your car some kid on the way home from junior choir practice might be tempted to steal it.

It's not that brokers are just grown-up kids who have to be watched, it's just that in their business, the devils of temptation come in giant sizes, and they do not whisper persuasions in the ear, they shout them.

If you give your broker permission to act as a principal in handling your account, you are asking for trouble. If you give him discretionary power—that is, if you run a *discretionary account* you're dangling bait before the nose of a sales representative. Likewise, if you buy your stock in a "Street name," and do not have it legally transferred to you, your broker may be forced, under financial stress, to misuse it to your loss or disadvantage.

A great many people, for one reason or another, think that a broker will "make money for me" if he is given a discretionary account, and allowed, with power of attorney, to make any trades that he may wish. Experience shows that the one who is sure to profit from a discretionary account is the broker. He makes commissions both ways, buying or selling, and with blanket authorization he usually keeps a discretionary account very active. The old professionals call this *boiling* or *churning*.

A discretionary account is set up usually when the investor has a substantial sum earmarked for the stock market and is too lazy or incompetent to handle his own portfolio.

This is done on the assumption that the broker knows more about investing than the investor does, which is not always the case. Brokers, it must be remembered, are really commission merchants who handle the buying and selling of property that they do not own. In many respects they are like real estate brokers, or insurance brokers. Some of the most successful real estate brokers care nothing, and know little, about building construction or land values. Stock brokers may know very little about the values of investing, or the art of advisory service and portfolio management. A broker usually has no training in analyzing stocks.

Discretionary accounts run to as little as one thousand dollars, but some have been recorded that were as high as a million dollars.

Opening a discretionary account is simply not a good investment practice—yet it's done all the time.

A common mistake, made frequently by widows, is to turn over a full-blown portfolio to the broker and ask him to manage it. A broker is not qualified to manage a portfolio, so he interprets this to mean that the investor wants him to run a discretionary account, giving him authority to buy or sell or switch as he sees fit. Since the broker's income is derived from buying and selling somebody else's stocks, he sees fit to exercise his discretionary powers whenever the opportunity presents itself. There are cases on record where a broker has traded as much as twice a day in the same discretionary account over a long period of time.

Brokers earn part of their income by selling from their own accounts. They buy a stock at a low price expecting that some corporate developments or special promotions will enhance its value. Then when it rises in price they try to sell it to their customers. If a broker is running a discretionary account for you, quite naturally you will "buy" some of his stock at the higher price.

If you do not have cash in the account—and no good broker is going to allow cash to accumulate in it—he will achieve your purchase by selling some stock that you own. This is called *switching*. It means that he switches your ownership from one stock to another.

Switching itself is a valid device employed by many traders, but

it's done for entirely different reasons. You'll find many sales result-
ing from switching at the end of the year when traders are conscious
of their taxes and, under some circumstances, may wish to take
losses.

Under a tax loss situation toward the year's end, a trader may
sell a stock on which he has suffered a loss and switch it into one
at a comparable price on which he expects substantial gains after the
beginning of the new tax year. This way he takes a loss in the current
tax year and postpones a profit until the next.

Another form of switching is on the profit side. Perhaps his
stock has gained all the points the trader expects, and he sells out
and buys another that he also thinks is on the way up.

Technically, a broker is supposed to let you know if he does any
switching in your account, but sometimes this information is slow
in coming. Also, it does little good to learn of a switch after the fact,
if you didn't want one in the first place.

Another area in which a broker with a discretionary account
can fleece the customer is by avoiding his *breakpoints*. A breakpoint
is the exact figure at which his commission drops to a lower category.
Obviously a broker is allowed to charge a higher commission *rate* on
a sale of a thousand dollars than he is on a sale of twenty-five
thousand dollars. His commission is a percentage of the selling price.

When he has discretionary powers, a broker may be tempted
to buy $24,900 worth of stock instead of $25,000, so he can charge
a higher rate, and if it is a security that ultimately increases in value
you'd regret not having bought the extra hundred dollars' worth.

It is easy enough to get cheated by an unscrupulous broker
when you are dealing with stocks on the New York Stock Exchange
or the American Stock Exchange, but when it comes to unlisted
securities, those traded over-the-counter, the opportunities for mis-
feasance and malfeasance are compounded.

Brokers who help to issue the stock of a new or a small corporation when it goes public, are usually owners of large blocks of the
original stock, and after the first blush of sales, are charged with the
task of *making a market*. This means, simply, that if too many people

want to sell, the broker is responsible for lining up a similar number of buyers to prevent the price from falling off, or he faces the prospect of buying the stock himself.

It is dangerous to leave a discretionary account with a broker who is involved in underwriting new over-the-counter issues or engaged in making a market for them. It is exceptionally convenient to place the unwanted stock of an embryonic company into a discretionary account.

Then, too, such an account is handy in case one of the original stockholders of a new company becomes disenchanted and wishes to sell a large block of his stock. The broker knows that if it were to be dumped onto the market, the price would tumble. Right at hand is your discretionary account which will buy the unwanted stock at the last market price, thus protecting it.

Another pitfall is when a broker is allowed to sell stock at a fixed price. This is permitted occasionally to allow the broker time to space out the sales of a new or a weak stock. In effect, for a limited time, he has the power to set the price on the security with total disregard to normal market pressures. A discretionary account is a convenient repository for such stock and it might give your portfolio a false value, for at the end of the broker's period of privilege for fixing the price, the stock might sell off considerably.

The point is, it is unlikely that you would be trading in such securities yourself, and it seems foolish, indeed, to allow your broker or any broker to act as principal in putting you into these situations.

On the other hand, much depends upon your broker, and how clever he is.

There is nothing illegal or even unethical about churning, switching or putting you into a stock in which the broker is dealing as principal if the results are beneficial to you.

If you are a good customer, a broker might well reward you for letting him make a market with your account by selling you out at a high point in the trading at good profit.

There is nothing that says a broker has to lose money for a client by churning and switching, either, and he might be clever enough to tack on some good profits for you as well as bolster his commissions.

Many discretionary accounts exist because their totals are too small to warrant professional supervision by a trained manager or advisor. Most investment counselors have a limit on what they will handle. Some will manage no portfolio valued at less than twenty-five thousand dollars. With others it's fifty thousand.

An investor with, say, ten thousand dollars to put into the market, reasons that he cannot afford to spend too much time with it, as there it has slim chance of yielding a sufficient return to pay for his effort. He then turns to his broker and authorizes him to trade it as a discretionary account.

Many men who have had long and pleasant, as well as profitable, relationships with a broker will arrange for a discretionary account to be left to their widows, believing that the broker will continue to perform good service. These fellows forget that brokers also die or retire or get sick, and that there's a good chance a total stranger will be handling the widow's discretionary account.

If you deem a discretionary account necessary to your own personal situation, either because you can't devote the time to your own portfolio or because it's too small to qualify for professional management, the best way to open one is to test out your broker.

You can do it by giving him discretionary powers over a small portfolio, say one thousand or two thousand dollars, and then watch him carefully over the next few weeks to see how it develops. If he has managed it without too much churning and switching, you can add some capital to the account.

But the cardinal rule with any discretionary account is to demand reports of what's going on. Ask your broker to send you a record of activity in your account each day that there is a transaction.

Most of the better brokerage houses will do this automatically, but you'd be surprised how many don't. No one will be offended if you ask for a *per diem* updating each time there is any activity in your account.

If you have a good broker who seems solidly professional and who is active in new underwritings and such, it may even be a good idea to let him have a discretionary account with some part of your investment portfolio, just to see if, when he has the right to act without your instructions, he will put you in on some of the newer goodies that come along from time to time.

Again, everything depends upon the broker.

Some kids, it is assumed, *can* be trusted alone in a candy store.

But this assumes, of course, that you can *afford* to run a test case on your broker to find out how he performs without your instructions. It is a risk.

By far the best, wisest and safest procedure for handling any account is to turn it over to an investment manager. These experts are registered with the Securities and Exchange Commission and are governed by regulations that are enforced by the Investment Counselors Association of America, a self-policing organization.

There are investment advisors who do not belong to the Association or who are not listed by the Association, if, for instance, they been dropped from the list for some infraction. You can check on the membership of any advisor or counselor by writing to the Association at 49 Park Avenue, New York, N.Y., 10016. The Association will send you a list of its members.

Investment advisors customarily charge you one-tenth of one percent of the market value of the stock you hold at the beginning of the year, or at the start of the management of your portfolio. They are not concerned with any other commissions. They are not affiliated with any stock brokerage operations.

Thus, if you had a portfolio that was valued at fifty thousand dollars on January first, your investment advisor would get a fee of fifty dollars for the year for telling you what stocks to buy and when to sell. For this tiny percentage of the action, you cannot blame the professionals for refusing to take on a portfolio of less than, say, twenty-five thousand dollars, which would yield a fee of only twenty-five dollars for a year's expert supervision.

Lacking the capital to get expert advice on your portfolio, the best thing to do is to handle it yourself. As pointed out in earlier chapters, there is plenty of source material for good and reliable information. One copy of the *Wall Street Transcript*, which carries the recommendations of market researchers, will give you a pretty good idea of the scope of subject matter covered in any one week.

If you say that you haven't got time to manage your own portfolio (if it's less than fifty thousand dollars in value) you should forget about investing and buy Treasury Notes, Savings Bonds or some good Municipal Bonds or, if you don't want to be bothered even that much, just put your money in a Savings Bank and return this book and get your money back—you may need it.

XXI *Why Buy Stocks, Anyway?*

There comes a point in the life of every investor when he wonders if he is doing the right thing. Perhaps his money would be better off in a savings bank. Or how about bonds—nice, secure government bonds? Or real estate—John Jacob Astor is credited with saying that nobody could ever get rich without investing in real estate, and went on to prove the truth of that adage for himself.

There are many places where you can put money and call it an investment: antiques, art, diamonds, gold bullion (if you keep it abroad), shorefront property, bonds of many varieties, savings accounts, old coins, stamps, and so on, *ad infinitum.*

The question is twofold:

1. Where do you get the most for your money?
2. Where is it safest?

Generally speaking, the person who invests in good common stocks gets the most for his money, and at the same time sacrifices little safety for the privilege. There are massive records to back up the claim.

Stocks are known to be just about the best hedge against inflation, ranking with or above real estate. What may be overlooked is the fact that inflation in the modern world is an almost constant factor, turning into deflation only in times of severe depression. What is involved in an investment decision is not whether there will be inflation, but *how much* inflation there will be.

Real estate increases in value in times of inflation, of course, but holding it may be a costly proposition these days, as all three of the taxing authorities, federal, state and local, search for higher revenues. Real estate is one of their prime targets. When profit is realized on real estate, it is taxable as a capital gain.

(If you sell your home and re-invest in another home, the amount of profit realized on your sale is *not* taxable—but then, it isn't real profit, either, since you must re-invest it in another dwelling with, presumably, an equally inflated price tag on it. Any amount of equity from the sale of your home that is not re-invested in another home, *is* taxable at a capital gains rate.)

Bonds, which pay a fixed rate of interest, have a capacity for losing money for you in two ways when inflation is severe. If you pay one thousand dollars for a bond that yields five percent interest, you expect to receive fifty dollars. If, however, inflation causes a price rise of five percent during the year, your capital will shrink to the equivalent of $950, and the interest that you receive will be worth not fifty dollars but $48.50 in purchasing power.

The same holds true for money kept in a savings account. The loss in purchasing power can wipe out whatever interest you receive, and at the same time it can debase the capital that you have saved, making it worth less to you.

If you are investing to supplement your income, you must regard your investment as a *worker* whose income should rise with inflationary pressures.

It is obvious that doctors, lawyers, accountants, gardeners, garbage collectors, auto mechanics, appliance repairmen and all others raise their fees and charges when inflation bites into their incomes. So do government employees, including policemen, firemen and school teachers. Those who work for companies or corporations also strive for higher wages and salaries to overcome the effects of inflation.

What of the investor? Where does he turn? He can't strike. He can't *demand* a greater return on his investment. He can't threaten the market with boycott or bruises if it doesn't yield him more profit.

The truth is, if he's in common stocks he doesn't have to resort to any such measures. The stock market compensates for inflation. In fact, it *over*-compensates.

For the decade 1951 through 1960, the prices of all stocks listed on the New York Stock Exchange rose 224 percent, while the cost

of living during that same decade, increased by twenty-three percent.

In the most recent decade, 1961 through 1970, the prices of
stocks on the New York Stock Exchange increased by fifty-four
percent while the cost of living was boosted by thirty-one percent.

This figure is for *appreciation* in the value of investment only.
It has nothing to do with dividends paid during those years.

And there's another side to the dividend story. The price of
stock is intimately related to the dividend paid by the company.
That is, if the dividend isn't high enough or constant, the price of
the stock will tumble in the marketplace.

Therefore it behooves the corporations to keep their dividends
as high as is prudent and consistent with good business management.
In the long run you may expect an appreciation in dividends as the
price of the stock reaches new and higher levels, if you have chosen
your company wisely.

The rate of yield you get on common stock, of course, depends
mainly on the price that you paid for it. If you buy stock for a
hundred dollars that is paying a six dollar dividend, you have a yield
of six percent. It makes no difference if the value of the stock
increases to $110 per share. If the company continues to pay six
dollars, your yield is still six percent. And if the stock drops to ninety
dollars, your yield is still six percent.

On balance, the ability of bonds to keep abreast of inflationary
movements is just about half as good as that of common stocks,
according to a study of a forty-year period by the University of
Chicago.

Common stocks are not absolutely riskless, of course. The market can—and does—fall. There *are* recessions when inflation is no
longer a severe or serious factor. There remains the fact, however,
that a common stock loss is not a real monetary loss until the stock
is sold. If you hold onto your stock during a bear market, you have
lost nothing, except on paper. And if your dividend rate remains
unchanged, your yield holds up and, in fact, is worth more in purchasing power.

In the long run, your stock is likely to appreciate in value if you have bought shares in a company that meets all other requirements.

The thing to remember about modern recessions is that they are neither long nor deep. They do not last as long as they once did, nor does the economy recess or depress as much as it once did.

This is probably due in most part to the creation and passage of the Full Employment Act of 1946 which charges the President with direct responsibility for using the government's resources to forestall or limit recessions. The same act established the President's Council of Economic Advisers, a group of economic experts whose responsibility it is to spot the onset of a recession before it occurs.

No President has been as completely successful as the creators of the act envisioned (the late Henry Wallace was a prime mover in getting it onto the books) but since its passage, recessions have been short-lived and shallow. One major reason the government has not been as successful as it might have been is that the President, in each case, was reluctant to begin pump-priming expenditures until the recession became a fact rather than a threat. Because there have been inflationary pressures in the economy at the same time, the President, in each instance, has feared to open the gates of government spending.

Recessions have occurred five times since the Full Employment Act became effective. There was one under Truman; there were three under Eisenhower and one under Nixon. The drop in industrial production has averaged out at ten percent, compared to nearly twenty percent in earlier recessions. On average, they last less than a year, compared to more than a year-and-a-half for the earlier ones.

It is obvious, then, that the power to end recessions must be provided by the government, and it is done with money. When a recession threatens, the government spends more money in an effort to forestall it. This, of course, may be inflationary, but if you are safely invested in common stocks, the inflation will affect you adversely only when you buy something; it will not deteriorate your investments.

Where it can hurt, however, is in your dividends. The government only gets money to spend from taxes. Corporations now pay nearly half of the tax revenues collected by Uncle Sam each year. If more money is needed, it will likely come from corporations rather than from individuals, since individuals feel the pinch of inflation more than corporations do. (Corporations can raise their prices to compensate.) It follows that any increase in corporate taxes will result in a decrease in corporate profits, and this, of course, relates directly to the dividend paid to stockholders.

You will know in plenty of time, however, if corporate taxes are to be boosted. There will be black headlines, and many pained outcries. The corporate world is not noted for its silence when government seeks to inhibit the profit rate.

Another thing to remember about any new tax the government might propose is this: Unless it's an excess profits tax for businesses only, it will have to be a boost in the capital gains tax, and that will also affect you directly whenever you trade your stock for a profit.

What this boils down to, essentially, is that there is *some* risk that America's phenomenal industrial growth will no longer be allowed to translate itself into corporate and business profits, but will be channeled off into taxes, ending the system that has brought wealth to so many investors in the past.

As an investor, then, you have a vested interest in the *status quo* of the tax structure, and it is to your advantage to let your representatives in Congress know of your feelings. Otherwise some innovative politician may inadvertently remove the last real hedge against the inflation that has characterized the American economy since the Revolution when the lyricist for *Yankee Doodle* complained, ". . . And what they wasted every day, I wish it could be sav-ed."

The price of stocks—their value—has been moving steadily higher since the beginning of this century, interrupted only by the crash of 1929 and the bottoming out of the market in 1932.

This, no matter how it's viewed, is a remarkable record. Old companies die and new ones are born. Existing products disappear and new and better ones come along. Many of the great corporations survive, despite product changes, management changes and ownership changes, seemingly as separate entities with lives of their own. Anyone who bought a thousand dollars' worth of the first issue of William C. Durant's General Motors stock in 1908 would today be worth many millions of dollars.

America's growth record is unmatched in all history in all of the world. Owning a share of common stock is buying into a piece of the action. Non-owners of common stock are missing a good share of the excitement that is part of the American way of life.

But it is not for emotional or patriotic reasons that an investor is wise to own common stocks. The record shows that the enhancement of investment values throughout this century has at least equalled and usually exceeded all others.

In addition to all the other inducements for owning common stocks, the fact is that they are usually liquid and can be bought or sold almost at will. A broker can usually find a buyer for your stock within a few minutes of your notification to sell.

There is no haggling about price—it is determined by what is usually a very accurate auction process. You don't have to search for a dealer to handle your sale. By looking in your daily newspaper's stock listings you can get a pretty good idea of what your sale price will be even before you give the order.

With almost everything else—diamonds, antiques, paintings, stamps, coins, even automobiles—you buy at retail, but when it comes time to sell, you dispose at wholesale.

Not so with stocks. You buy in a retail market and sell in a retail market, the most highly organized and militantly policed market in the world.

XXII *Don't Invest Too Much*
—Or Too Little

As of this writing more than 33 million Americans are believed to be owners of common stocks of American corporations. Some of them shouldn't be in the market. On the other hand, there are many millions more who *should* be investors, and who are not.

If you've read this far into this book it's a safe bet that you are already in the market or are thinking seriously of buying some common stock. Quite likely, if you analyzed your reasons for wanting to buy common stocks, they would come out this way:

1. You believe the stock is going to increase in price (value) in the future.

2. You believe it will pay you a reasonable dividend in the interim.

3. You believe it is a safe haven for your savings.

4. You believe that if inflation erodes too much value from the dollar, your common stock will adjust upward in value to compensate for it.

All other reasoning aside, the main purpose of your foray into the stock market is to make money, and to do so with the least possible risk.

In all that welter of securities there is a stock waiting just for you. All you need to do is identify it and buy it.

This stock has safety—it won't decline in price—it pays a liberal dividend—more than you could get for your money in a normal savings program, and it is absolutely destined to rise in price.

That, in essence, is the stock you're seeking, isn't it? You really don't care if it's a company that is in chemicals, automobiles, metals, drugs or aircraft. What you want is a stock that will make money for you, and do it at minimum risk.

As we've mentioned before, if you're looking for a speedy and sensational rise in the price of your stock, you have to more or less ignore the safety feature. It is likely to be a riskier stock than most, for the one that is capable of posting great gains is equally liable to post great losses. If you're seeking safety in your investment, the hoped-for rise in price may be inhibited by the stolidity of the issue you are forced to choose.

So you spend time and effort seeking the *right* stock for you. It is there; you *know* it's there, someplace. In one stock there are all the elements you need; safety, a good dividend income, assurances of a gain in price.

You can stop looking, Pilgrim. The stock you seek doesn't exist. It's not on the list on the New York Stock Exchange, the American Stock Exchange, the National Exchange, or anywhere else.

What you're looking for is not a solitary stock, it's a *group* of stocks, and it's called your *portfolio.* You want one kind of stock that will be very solid and stable. You want another that will pay a fair dividend. You want a third that is speculative and might possibly take off like a skyrocket. You may even want a fourth that combines some of the elements, perhaps one that pays a good dividend but is considered a candidate for a sudden rise in the future.

What you're lacking is an investment goal.

What your goal is to be depends entirely on your individual circumstances. These include the amount of money you have to invest, your prospects for earning more money to be added to your investments, your job outlook, your marital status, the number of dependents you have, their ages (how long will they be your dependents?) and many other factors, not the least of which may be your own health.

Upon reflection you will decide that there are many other people in exactly your circumstances who are successful and relaxed investors in the stock market. Your assignment, then, is to find out what they did about their portfolios and how they solved the identical problems that plague you now and will bother you in the future.

Rid yourself of the notion that most successful investors are New Yorkers; they're not. Or that you have to be in constant contact with Wall Street, for you don't.

Let's look at some typical American investors and see how they make their marketing decisions.

Young Couple, Modest Income

Bill and Mary Jones live in a middle-income suburb outside of Detroit. Bill operates an internal grinding machine in one of the large factories and brings home about nine thousand dollars a year when you count in his overtime and other supplemental work such as doing setting-up work on holidays and days off.

Through careful management the Joneses have raised two children to junior high school age, they've bought their own home, and they maintain an active savings account into which weekly deposits are made.

Now in their mid-thirties they have decided the time has come to invest in the stock market. The reasons for this are three-fold. First, Bill has learned that he is moving up to be foreman of his section at the beginning of the month, and this will mean an additional fifteen dollars a week in his pay envelope; second, their mortgage is just about paid off, and this will give them an additional sixty-five dollars a month to utilize in other ways; and third, their savings account has grown to two thousand dollars.

Thus, the situation is that they have two thousand dollars saved up and they face the prospect of having an additional $1,500 per year either to save or to invest. More insurance doesn't seem practical to Bill Jones. He has a policy of ten thousand dollars and also receives many benefits, including death and pension benefits, from his union.

Bill has read books on the stock market and is convinced that, aside from buying real estate, which he has already done, the best way to build an estate is through investment in common stocks.

Because he hasn't much money to put into the market, Bill Jones is looking for security—stock that is protected against a loss in price. In the first place, he decided that Detroit Edison looked good to him. His local utility is bound to grow, he thought, it had a reasonable debt structure, and paid reliable dividends. Those dividends would help reduce his own utility bill.

That's how he started. Then he commenced a Monthly Investment Plan, first buying ten shares of a consumer financial company, as it offered both security and a good growth potential, and then ten shares of a large and well-established chemical manufacturing company, because it, too, combined the twin elements of security plus growth potential.

Bill Jones now has a well-rounded portfolio and next time he starts buying on the MIP, he's going to get into something a little more volatile and just a bit riskier, but embodying a potential for greater gains. He may try one of the newer electronic company stocks to add a little spice to his holdings.

Young Couple, Higher Income

Charlie and Ethel Smith have clawed their way up the stony sides of Manhattan's challenge until now it seems to them they are in the tower suite. Charlie has been the highly successful Associate Editor of his magazine for six years, earning thirty thousand dollars a year.

They are buying a fifty thousand dollar home on Long Island's North Shore, and a hundred thousand dollar insurance policy, along with two cars, a small power boat and a mowing tractor for their lawn.

Surprisingly their savings account is only half as large as Bill Jones's.

You see, by the time Charlie and Ethel get through paying for their house, their insurance, and all the luxuries necessary for them to maintain their proper position in their suburban society, there isn't much left over to go into the bank. In fact, Charlie's equity in his house and the paid-up amount of his insurance policy are about all the Smiths have in the way of wealth.

That, plus Charlie's highly promising job.

And now Charlie has learned that the editor is going to retire and he will be promoted to the top editorial post at an increase in salary of ten thousand dollars a year.

First, the limousine must be replaced. It is now three years old. And Ethel's mink is positively shameful, it is so out-of-style. And speaking of clothes, Charlie wants to visit that tailor in Toronto and order a half-dozen suits. After all, he'll be needing them. Not to be forgotten, either, is the fact that about a thousand dollars must be put aside for a celebration party marking Charlie's ascendency to the top spot on the magazine.

Even so, there'll be some money left and Charlie told Ethel that it is high time they thought about buying some stocks. Why, he heard a fellow on the train the other morning talking about a new electronic computer company that was going so far as to build systems for computerizing library cards.

Just imagine how much money that company was destined to make. He would, Charlie resolved, ask the fellow-passenger for the name of that company and they might get in on the ground floor with a little stock purchase now.

No, Ethel said. They needed something secure and safe and *conservative*. Suppose there should be sickness. After all, they still had two young children who could develop some dreadful disease or be injured while romping around the bay. They needed some kind of cash protection. What they really needed, Ethel said, was cash in the bank and at least half of the ten thousand dollar raise should go into the savings account each year. If not there, Ethel said, it should go into government bonds.

Ethel was right. A bit too severe, perhaps, but right nevertheless.

In the end, they decided to buy three thousand dollars worth of Treasury Notes, a form of Government bond, and to invest one thousand dollars in a deep blue chip (they selected United States Steel), and to add one thousand dollars to their savings account. They decided that they would save their major investing program for next year, when they could more fully appreciate the added benefits of Charlie's raise.

And then, they decided, they would seek security and dividends, because when you really analyzed it, they didn't need the profit from growth stocks. They had plenty of income. What they really wanted was security. And that's how they framed their investment policy.

Young Conservative Couple

We come now to Jim Adams, age thirty-eight and his wife, Betty, and their two children, who are in their late teens, both in college. Jim Adams is a corporation lawyer, a partner in one of the most respected law firms in the area.

The Adamses' life together is the result of careful planning. Jim's income is now thirty-five thousand dollars a year, but it wasn't always that way. When he started out it was fifty dollars a week, and that followed long years of expense at law school. Jim waited four long years before marrying Betty, until his annual income was assured at ten thousand dollars, and their first home was carefully chosen in a nearby suburb—small, just right for a young couple with possibly one child, and in the path of suburban growth so that its value was likely to increase.

Later, when their second child arrived, Jim was making twenty thousand dollars a year and they were able to move into the house they now occupy, which was really far beyond the means of a twenty-thousand-dollar-a-year lawyer because Jim had so much equity in the small house he was selling they were able to buy it. Jim knew that he was buying for the future, and that it would pay him to tighten his belt a bit while he was young in order to get the fine quality home in an excellent neighborhood that he would want when he became more affluent.

Jim has lived in that home now for ten years and the mortage is nearly one-third paid. Monthly payments are no problem to him.

Jim also has a hundred thousand dollar life insurance policy on which he has been paying for ten years. It was an open-ended policy and he started it at twenty-five thousand dollars fifteen years ago, and raised it to fifty thousand a couple of years later, and to a hundred thousand ten years ago, matching this program to his progress in the firm and the increases in his income.

The Adamses drive the heavier model of a medium-priced car, which they consider luxurious, and he has a six-year-old hand-shift Volkswagen that he drives to the station and leaves in the commuters' parking lot.

There is five thousand dollars in the Adams savings account, a constant balance of $1,500 in their checking account. They pay their Federal Income Tax in estimated quarterly increments and always tender a carefully prepared return that guarantees them a modest refund from the government.

Expenses are limited to the membership dues in the country club and the summer rental of a home in the Berkshires, where the family spends the season and Jim relaxes for a month. Two years ago Jim negotiated an option to buy the place so that any year he decides to buy it, that summer's rent will apply to the purchase price.

When he was twenty-five years old, Jim Adams bought his first share of common stock. It was actually ten shares. He bought Consolidated Edison. He put the shares away in the safe deposit box and vowed he would forget them, implying that he was really buying them for the sake of his children or grandchildren. He didn't really forget them, but he left them alone, and has to this day.

Jim has the advantage of receiving a substantial part of his pay as a year-end distribution of partnership earnings. He calls it his "bonus," though it is really a distribution of earnings to which he is entitled.

It forces him to live at a level of thirty-thousand dollars all year through, and then suddenly come into five thousand dollars that doesn't have to be applied to basic living expenses. Some years ago he fell into the habit of putting a large portion of his bonus money into common stocks.

Jim, as a corporate lawyer, had handled some utility cases and had become convinced that utilities offered about the safest and yet most promising stocks on the market. Accordingly, he looked for utility issues in localities where there seemed to be a good growth potential. He bought L. I. Lighting, Rockland Power & Light, Florida Power Company and Illinois Bell, in successive years, and some years he added to his existing holdings.

This year he intends to buy some more utility stock, but hasn't made up his mind which one it will be. He is looking at the records of companies in Arizona and California.

Under his particular circumstances Jim Adams has handled his affairs well. He has a hang-up, however, over utilities, simply because many of his stocks are "safe." It is now time for him to get into more glamorous fields and balance out his portfolio. He should look to the surgical supply or electronic industries, perhaps, for a small investment of this year's bonus. A good medical and drug supply company might provide him with some growth potential that is lacking in his present portfolio.

This is not to say he should sell any of his fine utilities for the sake of diversification. Rather, he should pride himself on the solid base of his portfolio, and go on from there with something slightly more speculative, with, perhaps, the potential for a greater gain in value. He has built well and thoughtfully, and now is the time to experiment a little bit.

Jim cannot afford to be reckless. Law firms do have their ups and downs, just as does any other business. He has two children to put through college. There is always the spectre of possible illness with enormous costs. But as a night out with the boys may be beneficial to the soul, so a little harmless fling in the stock market may broaden and brighten the sturdy and stolid portfolio that he now possesses.

Young Man, Single

Let's back down the ladder a bit to consider the case of David Miller, age twenty-seven, unmarried, a college graduate, a navy veteran and a traffic control man in the headquarters office of a large appliance manufacturer. He has received several compliments from his boss and is considered a "comer."

David lives with his parents in a nice suburb. His income is eight thousand dollars a year, and he knows that he will be making more next year, and, if he does his job well will be promoted every year or two. His employer is a large corporation, noted for its ability to get the most out of its employees and reward them accordingly. He faces the future with confidence. Even so, he has decided to remain single for some time to come. He hasn't found "the" girl.

Without quite planning it that way, David already has an estate. He has a ten thousand dollar National Service Life Insurance policy that he converted from term to ordinary life after he was discharged from the navy. In addition, there's a five thousand dollar group policy at his work. From his first year's earnings, he has saved $2,500, since he pays his parents only thirty dollars per week for room and board, and doesn't spend much on other activities. He had an additional $2,500 saved up from his years in the navy, so he has five thousand dollars in cash savings, and no real responsibilities.

Aside from the fact that David Miller might like to buy a car to get away from home weekends, and perhaps meet that girl, he realizes that he has too much in cash.

David should leave one thousand dollars in his savings account and continue his program of thrift. The remainder, four thousand dollars, should go to start a well-balanced portfolio. He might buy some stock in the company where he is employed. It is a big appliance manufacturer, but it is also a prime industrial producer, making generators, elevators, locomotives, aircraft engines, light bulbs and many other things for consumers around the world.

Its stock might fluctuate a bit with the tides of the industrial economy, but it is a sound corporation and has survived many economic storms so that, to the professional analysts, it is regarded as a "defensive" stock.

He might then add a good blue-chip stock to his portfolio, possibly a solid public utility. With the remainder, however, he can well afford to speculate. Not much damage can befall him, even if his stock tumbles severely. He might try some of the aircrafts, or drugs, or medical supplies, or electronics companies.

What he should be looking for, of course, is good growth stock, and the market is full of them—some better than others. It is also well supplied with growth stocks that will never grow, so he must move carefully into the area of speculation.

But that still leaves David Miller with some additional investment responsibility—the $2,500 that he manages to save each year out of his salary. It, too, should be invested in part. For safety, he may wish to add five hundred dollars per year to his savings account, but, since his responsibilities are limited, the remaining two thousand dollars should go into the investment of good stocks.

David doesn't receive his $2,500 in a lump sum. He gets paid every other week, and he saves a portion of that paycheck. There are three ways he can divert that money into investments:

1. He can continue to save it at his bank and make stock purchases when he believes the market is right. This way he earns maximum interest for unescrowed savings, and by purchasing his stock in round lots, he pays lower commissions.

2. He can join a Monthly Investment Plan with his broker and make monthly purchases through the regular MIP procedures.

3. He can deposit his savings with his broker to hold until such time as he is ready to make a stock purchase. This is less expensive than the MIP plan because it permits the broker to buy stocks in either round lots or odd lots, without dealing in fractional shares.

The Executive Secretary

Phyllis Johnson is thirty-five years of age and considered highly successful as executive secretary of a top executive officer in a large corporation. She makes $150 a week, lives alone in a prim but adequate apartment, maintains a good business wardrobe, and generally lives modestly. She is a childless widow. Her husband was killed in an automobile accident, leaving her with some life insurance which she used, wisely, to finish her education.

Phyllis saves about $1,200 a year at the rate of a hundred dollars per month, and now has nearly five thousand dollars, all of it in an ordinary savings account drawing day-of-deposit–day-of-withdrawal interest, which is about the lowest rate the banks pay.

Now Phyllis is convinced she should buy some stocks—but *which* stocks? Actually, Phyllis's needs are small. She has a five thousand dollar life insurance policy, which names her comfortably situated parents as beneficiaries. She has hospital insurance and major medical policies at work. She is in good health, happy at her job and happy with her life. She is dated frequently by eligible bachelors, but has no plans for re-marrying.

Leaving a thousand dollars in the bank for emergencies, Phyllis should consider putting her money into a few shares of a wide variety of blue chips, ranging, say, from General Electric or Westinghouse, to the food processors, the food chains, some Standard Oil of California or other good petroleum, some auto stocks, and at least one good utility.

This will give her a good solid base from which to operate. After purchasing these diversified blue chips, she might look for growth situations, being willing to sacrifice some safety for the potential gains.

An ideal way to do this would be through the Monthly Investment Plan, where she could afford to put seventy-five dollars, reducing to twenty-five dollars the monthly amount she puts into her savings account.

The Establishment Man

Ed Bosworth complains that his feet hurt. He is fifty-five years old and he frequently says, jokingly, that he doubts that he'll make it to retirement. He has been with his company for thirty years in the selling end of the business, and lately he has been assigned to writing sales reports, a job he hates.

He has confided to his wife, Bertha, his suspicions that the new, young president, fresh from the ranks of a strong competitor, and now firing up Ed's organization, doesn't like him and would like to force him into early retirement. Ed knows that his age would preclude his getting a job elsewhere, and he also knows that he can't just walk in and quit without losing his retirement benefits.

He is forced to remain at his post and undergo the indignities of writing reports, sweating it out for perhaps three or four years, until the new man at the top gets around to firing him. By then, Ed will be nearing sixty, with no shred of a chance for getting another job.

Ed has been making twenty thousand dollars a year for a number of years (since back there when it counted) plus a bonus of one or two thousand each year, depending on his sales. He has a savings program that is worth fourteen thousand dollars, some of it in Government Series "E" bonds, some in savings, some in a savings and loan association.

His mortgage is paid off. His children are grown and married. He has a forty-thousand dollar life insurance policy with low premiums, since it has been in force since he was age twenty-five. He also knows that if he hangs on until the boss fires him, he will get half of his pension, which will amount to about five hundred dollars per month for life. It's not what he expected, but it's not bad.

The problem is—can he turn that fourteen thousand dollars savings into something that will tide the gap until he turns 65 and can supplement his pension with Social Security?

He should be able to. A portion, of course, should be left in savings for emergencies—perhaps two thousand dollars. He may then get some additional cash from his insurance policy. He doesn't really need forty thousand dollars in life insurance. Bertha should be able to do nicely on twenty-five thousand if something should happen to him.

Then, with some careful shopping, he should be able to find the stocks that have safety (for he can't afford to lose at this point in life) plus good growth potential. The chemicals come to mind. Also the automobile companies. Also some of the natural resources companies. Also some of the companies with good records in the field of research and merchandising.

Ed Bosworth should be able to increase his capital substantially during the next three or four years, and be a fairly independent and free agent by the time the axe falls.

The Retired Couple

Mr. and Mrs. Walt Oliver are both over sixty-five and retired. Walt gets a small company pension and they receive Social Security. Their total monthly income is $225 a month. Their only other assets consist of their home in Florida, which they own free and clear (having sold their home in Wisconsin after their retirement and bought this one), plus about forty-five thousand dollars in savings, most of it realized from cashing in on insurance policies that Mr. Oliver had purchased over the years. A small, paid-up five thousand dollar policy remains in force on Mr. Oliver's life.

The couple pays a small, reduced premium for health insurance that includes major medical care and hospitalization.

Catherine Oliver has been urging Walt to do something about that large savings account, thinking he should be able to get more money out of it than the interest paid by the bank. Walt, in his traditional role as provider, resisted the notion of tampering with it. He believes conservation of his money is of paramount importance at his age.

Mr. Oliver has conceded, however, that some money might be put into preferred stocks that would yield them as much or perhaps more than the savings and loan pays in interest.

Mrs. Oliver said that was still too conservative, and that they should consult a good advisor.

So they did. They paid an advisor a flat fee to go over their affairs and make suggestions as to what they should do.

They didn't need quite so much safety, their advisor told them. What they needed, instead, was a little more risk to provide higher dividends and possibly a profit on some of the stock they owned.

He suggested that, since they were assured of a pension and Social Security anyway, and there was no threat that they would lose their home, they should put thirty-six thousand dollars into good dividend-paying stocks that seem to have a potential for growth. Some of those he named were blue chips; some were defensive stocks; some were newer "glamour" stocks.

His original suggestion was to put six thousand dollars into each of six such stocks. On reflection, he named two or three stocks in each category, and suggested that they put three thousand dollars into some issues.

Named by the advisor were good companies in these fields— mining, petroleum, natural gas, chemicals, automobiles, and steels.

These are cyclical stocks that reflect more closely than most the changes in the business cycle. They have a record for posting good dividends in good years—up to ten or even twelve percent, and for appreciating in price value by twenty to fifty percent.

Only a few of the issues the Olivers bought had to perform that well to substantially improve their position.

"You know", observed Walt Oliver one night at supper, "I've learned that it's not always safest in a bank."

"And it isn't always put to its full use in a bank," Catherine Oliver added.

Perhaps you may find yourself in one of the situations outlined in the foregoing. Perhaps you are, however, untypical, and need some special treatment in the stock market.

The purpose of this chapter is to show that there are a great variety of stocks in the market and they can be purchased in an infinite number of combinations to serve an elaborate number of needs.

The trick is to know what you need to serve you best—and then to set about finding it. If you look hard enough, you will be able to find it.

The market is big enough for everyone.

XXIII *Cliches That May Throw You*

If you get sick, there will always be plenty of people to give you advice even if they don't know an aspirin from an amphetamine. The minute you enter the stock market you may subject yourself to the legion of amateur advisers who mouth the same platitudes over and again. They believe it makes them seem wise. If you agree with them, you may find yourself in trouble, for a good share of their advice is extremely unwise.

The *one* platitude that you should remember is: *Advice is cheap.* It is, if you don't take it. If you heed the advice of amateurs, you may find it very expensive. The other old saw, *You get what you pay for,* applies most accurately to market advice. If you buy your advice from a legitimate, licensed adviser, it will at least be worth what you pay for it, and quite likely, more. If you get your advice for nothing—that is most likely what it will be worth.

Keeping up with the amateur advice-givers, Wall Street itself has evolved a whole compendium of cliches that apply to almost every conceivable market situation, and you are bound to hear them proclaimed, usually in stentorian tones, and generally as though they had been handed directly from the top of Mount Sinai.

Following are a few of them you probably will encounter:

The market always turns lower on good news. Strangely, this seems to be the case quite often. This cliche is a tribute to the market's ability to *discount* news in advance.

Suppose, for instance, the President calls a White House conference to make an announcement of momentous proportions—for example, that the war had ended. More often than not, the traders on Wall Street will have anticipated this news for days in advance and have run up the prices of stock in advanced active bidding. Then, when the news finally breaks, the normal reaction will be to sell the inflated stock at a cash profit.

When the industrials are off, the utilities will gain. Here's another one—like most of them—with some strong elements of truth. Again, it isn't *always* true, particularly in day-to-day or week-to-week trading. In the long range trend of the market, if industrials are soft and not attracting much investment money, that capital has to go somewhere, and it will seek out the safer stocks, those with long histories of dividends. The utilities beckon at such times because of their feature of safety. Their very dullness is attractive when the trend of the market seems uncertain to the investors.

Buy 'em when they're high and sell 'em when they're low. This is sound advice, handed down through the years. It is attributed to Bernard M. Baruch. It has only one thing wrong with it. How do you know when a stock is "low" or "high"? If it's lower than it has been in the past, it's low, but it may go lower still. Somehow it's even harder to determine when a stock is high. If you hold it one more day, it may go lower. If you sell it today, it may post some good gains tomorrow. The advice in this cliche is good, but the directions are vague. Mr. Baruch had his own crystal ball, and he didn't share it.

If you buy before Easter, sell before Christmas. This dates back to the beginning of the capital gains tax provision. It is fine-sounding advice if taxes are more important than anything else in your particular situation. Then, of course, the trick is to hold for at least six months, take your profit and get into something else that you can hold for at least six months. Of all the reasons why a stock should be sold, a tax reason is the saddest. Sadder than any, if viewed in a certain perspective, is the sale that is made by the calendar. This is a good cliche to forget.

If a stock rises in price before noon, it will fall before the closing bell. This happens a great many times, of course, but as an operating rule or acceptable adage, it is a lot of bunk. It is often the case that a stock which posts gains early in the day will be sold for quick profit by many of its owners before the market's close, but don't count on it. More often than not, gains will hold right through the trading session, all other conditions being equal.

Closely related to the foregoing is:

Stocks that gain late in the day will continue their gains the next day. A tiny grain of common sense enters this one. If upward price movement in a stock comes late in the day, accompanied by some good activity in the stock, it means that something has aroused interest, and it seems logical to assume that the interest will carry over to the next day. But this should concern you only if you have become a boardroom denizen and go in for a lot of in-and-out trading.

Broad-based conglomerates are best for newcomers because they offer diversity. They do offer diversity all right, but they are not always best for amateurs and newcomers to the market. There's more to stock ownership than diversity of the holdings. Sometimes, you know, conglomerates result from exceedingly poor management. A fellow who can't make a go of it in one industry, acquires a failing company in another industry to spread his losses. He runs a conglomerate all right, but he may be driving it straight toward the wall.

Insurance stocks are safer than any others. Many of the leading life insurance underwriters offer safe stocks all right, but they are not particularly safer than many utilities, some other financial institutions, and several industrials. This cliche originated in California where strict codes had to be drawn up for the handling of the earnings of child movie stars, and the creation of funds consisting of the stocks of insurance companies was sanctioned as safe. To find out the safest stocks (and there is no real guarantee of their safety), write to the New York State Banking Commissioner, 100 Church Street, New York, N.Y., and ask for the list of companies approved for stock investment for that state's mutual savings banks. The savings banks, with fiduciary responsibility for the investment of other people's money, may invest only in stocks that have been approved by the banking commissioner. If safety is what you want more than anything else, the list will interest you. Be prepared for a pretty dull time of it, though, for the stocks are selected for their glacial stability.

Always take your losses quickly. Well, if you must take a loss, do it manfully. Experience shows that a quick incision hurts the least. However, just because a stock is selling lower for a period of time doesn't necessarily mean that you must take a loss. We commonly believe that a stock's price is set in the open auction market by the inevitable forces of supply and demand, so it may be supposed that if a stock begins to sell lower for a period of time, the price reflects the opinion of the stock by the investing public. This is not necessarily so, particularly if a stock is closely held or narrowly held with the result that there is not too much normally available for the market. Then its price will be affected when one large investor seeks to divest himself of his holdings in the stock. This may have nothing to do with his evaluation of the stock—it may merely mean that he needs the money for something else, possibly something as remote as an alimony settlement. The point is, don't be stampeded. If you must take a loss, take it quickly, but don't be frightened into taking one that is unnecessary. The Crash of 1929 never would have occurred if everyone had held fast.

Buy when others are selling; sell when they are buying. This is a cliched version of the art of contrary opinion, and it is solid advice. You simply can't make money, though, if you spend your investing life bucking the trend of the market. If you had been selling stocks all through the bull market of recent years you wouldn't be very well off today. This particular piece of advice is for the short range view. Stay ahead of the public; don't merely oppose it.

Buy 'em and put 'em in the safe. Okay, but for how long? There have been innumerable articles written on how rich you would be if you had bought du Pont stock when it was first issued and held onto it through the years, or had bought General Motors when William C. Durant first brought it out, and had held onto it for all this time. True, true, but suppose you had bought Hudson Motor Car instead? Or Maxwell? In fact, if you had bought the most popular automotive stock at the time General Motors was being formed, you would have purchased Stutz Bear Cat, which filed for bankruptcy on December 31, 1929, two months after the big crash.

There is an element of good sense in the adage, of course, for it will pay you not to become excited about price fluctuations and to remain steadfast, as though your stock was, indeed, locked up in the safe. But by all means remain flexible. If you maintain a granite-like or arbitrary attitude about your investments, you may expose yourself to some losses, particularly over the long range. Conditions change. So do companies. So do products. As a result, so do profits.

Related to the above is:

Don't outwear your welcome in the market. This means, of course, don't stay too long with one stock. Again, it's a good piece of *general* advice, but it doesn't tell you when to sell and take a profit. How high is up? How long is too long?

Stand firm on strike news. Good advice. Why should you sell on news of a strike? If you've been paying attention, you have discounted a strike long before it's called, and so has the general investing public.

You won't go broke taking a profit. Aye, verily. Truer words were rarely uttered, but looked at candidly, this is a misleading axiom. While you certainly won't go broke by taking a profit, you may lose much added profit by taking it too quickly. The thrust of this old saw is to get you to turn over your stocks as soon as they show a little black ink for you. Don't be tricked into padding up the commission sales for brokers.

Buy transportation stocks in the Spring. Well, sure, if they appeal to you, but don't neglect them at other times of the year. The theory behind this old chestnut is that the transport companies make their most money in the summer months on vacation travel and such. This is no longer true, of course, if it ever was. In other times people would profit by buying stocks on a seasonal basis. It is said that the old farmers in Maine would buy Bangor & Aroostock Railroad in the late Summer because it would post its biggest profits in the Fall hauling potatoes to market, enhancing the value of the stock for the canny growers who would sell before first-quarter earnings, reflecting Winter's dull business, would depress prices. People are too sophisticated today, and ownership of stock is generally too broad, being held by both individuals and institutions that are disinclined to trade in and out so capriciously.

Take your profits on good news. There's logic here. Presumably, the prospect of good news has been discounted while it was still impending, and, having bought the stock before the good news was imminent, you appreciated some paper profit in the discounting. When the good news breaks, there's profit lurking that can be turned into cash.

Bulls and bears grow fat; hogs grow lean. In earlier chapters we have shown how both the bull and the bear—the optimist and the pessimist—can make money in the stock market, but this Wall Street proverb has to do with a third animal in the marketplace— the hog.

Let's face the fact that the desire to make money is what brings you into the market in the first place. It is not a shameful motivation, for it is the drive behind all business, everywhere. Even in the Soviet Union, the state must make a profit on whatever it produces and sells, and the manager who produces and sells the most becomes the most important bureaucrat.

Making a profit or making money is different, however, from greed. Greed can be destructive to the investor in the stock market. If you own a good stock that yields you a good return, you'd better think twice about dumping it for something that looks as though it might give you a better return. In the market, the greener pastures are usually circumscribed by a moat.

Don't speculate with investments. An investment, in the pure sense, is a *good* investment, one returning a fair percentage of gain to you and one with qualities that will let it grow in value over a certain period of time. If you have a good investment it is silly to sell it for the purpose of getting cash to put into a speculative venture, even though the venture may yield spectacular gains, *if* it turns out to be good. If it has got a wildly promising prospect, chances are it has a great deal of danger attached to it.

Odd-lot buyers can rarely win big. You hear this over and again in Wall Street and it is simply not true. The basis, of course, is that people who buy in odd-lots of less than a hundred shares just don't have enough capital to do it right. Moreover, they pay higher commissions for their transactions since they're not trading in round lots. The truth is, however, that the odd-lotters usually deal in the stocks that are the market leaders, and if you look back over three-quarters of a century and see how the leading stocks have performed, you'll see that the odd-lot traders did fine. If they didn't, it was not because they dealt in small quantities, but probably because, being amateurs, they made other mistakes.

XXIV *Over·the·Counter and Other Markets*

Nearly two-thirds of those who own stocks in America earn less than $7,500 a year, according to a survey compiled for the New York Stock Exchange, and more than one-third earn less than five thousand dollars annually.

While this is good, for it means that more people are participating in the functions of the capitalist system (as well as working in it), it also means that a great many people are forced to shop for bargains.

This is no doubt a sensible thing to do at Woolworth's or at the supermarket, particularly in times of inflation, but bargains are not always so apparent in the marketplace for securities. A shortage of cash available for the purchaser quite often sends him on a search among penny stocks, those low-priced issues traded in the Over-the-Counter market in the United States and on numerous foreign exchanges.

There are literally thousands of excellent stocks to be purchased in the Over-the-Counter market, and thousands of other highly qualified securities in the foreign exchanges, some of which may be purchased at attractively low prices. The pitfall lies in the fact that there are many thousands of low-priced stocks that are so highly speculative as to make absurd purchases for buyers in the lower income brackets.

These are far more suited to upper-bracket buyers who can afford to take tax losses, if that's what they turn out to be.

Because what we term "other exchanges" are actually legitimate auction markets or trading places, we will deal with them separately and consider first the much-discussed *Over-the-Counter* market.

This is not a place at all; it is a manner of doing business and a special way of matching bids to buy with offers to sell. It is a highly-organized market, carefully policed and supervised, and is governed by a complicated set of rules. It is how stocks are traded if they are not listed on an exchange.

A stock may not be listed on an exchange because it may be the security of a company that is not large enough or rich enough. On the other hand, it may not be listed on an exchange because even though it's big and rich, the company's ownership is narrowly held, or simply because it is company policy *not* to be listed.

The Over-the-Counter market is, in effect, the biggest market in the world, for it is there that you purchase the stock of any company that is not listed on any exchange—and they number into the tens of thousands, large and small, new and seasoned, many displaying great promise, others reflecting a brilliant past.

Strictly speaking, however, when a professional trader refers to the Over-the-Counter market he is discussing only those stocks that are listed in the quotation sheets of the National Association of Securities Dealers. The N.A.S.D. operates under strict rules specifically applying to the matching of bid and asked prices, and the making of a market to support the price of a stock, in somewhat the same way that a specialist does on a listing exchange that handles the auction trades of stocks that are listed with the exchange, and are publicly traded there.

When you trade in the market for unlisted securities, you are making an individual transaction with the dealer. He collects no commission. He makes—or hopes to make—a profit. Thus he is not acting as your agent, as your broker is when trading in your behalf in the markets of listed securities, such as the New York Stock Exchange. There the broker acts as your agent, trying to buy or sell something for you at the best possible price.

When you ask your broker to buy you an unlisted security,

however, he has to go to a securities dealer who handles such transactions, and there has to haggle over the price. If what you're buying
is an actively traded stock, the dealer will most likely know the exact
price at which he can sell and make a profit, and he'll make a quote
on a take-it-or-leave-it basis.

There is a sort of wholesale market in these unlisted securities,
so that one dealer may buy from another dealer in what is called the
inside market, probably at a half-a-point (fifty cents) or lower than
the public has to pay for it. If your dealer doesn't have the stock you
request, he will shop around among other dealers to get the best
price possible, and then quote you a price, with his profit added on.

Very frequently, such dealers carry inventories of a wide variety
of stocks, having bought them at wholesale for the inside market
price, and prepared to sell them at retail or the *outside price*.

This practice dates back to pre-revolutionary days, hence the
term that he sells Over-the-Counter. He handles stock as a commodity.

Ever since the Civil War, when contraband and black market
goods were sold "under the counter," the image-conscious securities
dealers of Wall Street have been trying to discourage use of the term
Over-the-Counter for transactions involving unlisted securities, but
to no avail. The term persists, and being precise, no doubt will
continue to do so in the future. Many public relations campaigns
notwithstanding, it is like trying to persuade a New York cab driver
to stop calling Avenue of the Americas Sixth Avenue.

Quite often you will hear a dealer say that what he sells is
"commission free," implying that the buyer is getting a bargain.
Sometimes the buyer does get a bargain, but just as often he pays
a bit more than he would if it were a commission sale.

When it comes to selling your unlisted stock, the dealer will
quote you a price that is anywhere from a half-point to a point under
the price that he can get for it by selling to the outside market. But
again, you pay no commission—just the stock transfer tax.

A dealer doesn't always buy your stock from you for purposes
of resale. Occasionally, he may decide to keep the stock for himself.

Perhaps he has had several inquiries about it lately. Possibly he thinks the dividend is going to be increased. Maybe he has reason to believe the stock will tack on a few points in the weeks or months ahead.

If he keeps the stock for inventory he is said to be *taking a position*. He has to report this fact to his regulatory officials.

If you take your stock to a dealer to be sold, chances are he will make a bee-line to the dealer who is taking a position in your stock, for most times that dealer will offer the best prices in town. He has to be careful not to let his enthusiasm carry him into a profitless position, however, for if he bids up his own stock, he'll make a profit on what he has in inventory, but he'll shut off his source of supply.

If the dealer really likes the stock and begins to trade in it for his own account, he is said to be *making a market*. In this function he is very much like the specialist on the New York Stock Exchange, for he can be counted on to meet reasonable demands to maintain an orderly market in the stock. He is expected to be willing to buy or sell the stock at any time, and to post publicly the prices at which he is willing to trade it. These will be in two sets of prices—the wholesale and the retail—the inside and the outside.

When a good dealer is making a market in a stock it has a narrow, conventional *spread*, on both the inside and outside markets. There may be only a point or two separating the bid price from the asked price.

If a stock is not well-known or well-favored, the spread may be greater.

The profit a dealer makes on a sale is determined by several factors, not the least of which is competition. If a number of dealers are making markets in the same stock, the prices of all of them are likely to be in line, and the profit margin will be narrow.

If you want to buy a stock that is inactively traded and the dealer has to shop around to find it, he will probably want a higher mark-up than he would on a stock that is in an active market.

The National Quotation Bureau is a private firm that daily publishes the inside price on thousands of Over-the-Counter stocks

in mimeographed "pink sheets." These are published in three different regional editions, Eastern, Western and Pacific Coast.

Each afternoon the dealer calls the National Quotation Bureau
and makes public the inside price of stocks in which he is making
a market. As best he can, he matches up the bids with the offers.
These prices are then quoted in the pink sheets and distributed to
dealers' offices throughout the country. In all probability your broker
will have the daily pink sheets and can give you the inside bid and
asked prices on any stock that has any reasonable trading activity.

Such quotations appear in abbreviated lists in the *Wall Street
Journal* and the *New York Times*. In each publication, extreme care
is taken to publish the quotes of stocks that are in most demand and
for which there is a legitimate market. Neither newspaper will list
a stock's quotations merely because a dealer wishes it, or because an
interested person in the company's management wants to have it
quoted. In other large newspapers around the country regional stocks
are similarly listed, along with those that have commanded national
attention.

The prices that you read in the newspaper, therefore, in the
Over-the-Counter list or list of Unlisted Securities, are inside prices,
the actual value, *per se,* of the stock. The price that you will have
to pay is slightly higher. But, again, there is no commission charge.
The stock transfer tax will be paid by the seller.

The effect of the pink sheets and of the published quotations
is to stimulate competition and to stabilize prices on the inside
market. This, in turn, makes for more uniform profit margins, so that
it rarely pays an individual to shop from dealer to dealer to get a
better price if the quotations have appeared in the sheets or in the
newspapers. This makes it to some extent self-regulating.

Let's suppose, however, that you formerly lived in San Francisco where you bought the stock of a local electronics manufacturing firm called, let's say, Jonesatron. Now, however, you are living
in New York, and you want to sell your Jonesatron stock. You go to
a reputable dealer in Wall Street and ask him to sell your hundred
shares.

The dealer's first chore will be to check local dealers to see if anyone will buy it. If none respond, he will then try Chicago, Denver, and ultimately San Francisco. If no dealer in San Francisco is trading in the stock, he will then call some of the banks to see if they have potential customers, and in the end may even call the Jonesatron company itself to induce the treasurer to buy the stock for the company's own account.

In the absence of any competition in the stock's market, the dealer has had to go to some lengths to dispose of your hundred shares of Jonesatron. How much are his services worth?

A regulation imposed by the National Association of Securities Dealers, the policing agency of the Over-the-Counter market, states that the profit margin should not exceed five percent of the sale price of the stock, unless special circumstances justify a greater charge.

If your stock were to sell for twenty dollars a share, the dealer could, within the regulations, charge you one point, netting you nineteen dollars a share. His profit would be one hundred dollars.

If he thought such hard salesmanship was worth more than a hundred dollars, he would have to contact you and get your agreement to a percentage greater than five percent. He would need this agreement in writing, to protect himself from action by the N.A.S.D.

We are exploring the Over-the-Counter market in depth because many of its low-priced stocks have allure for the small investor, and unless he knows exactly what is happening, he can be confused by it.

The size and scope of the OTC market is unknown. Its operations are much larger than the New York Stock Exchange, and are probably larger than all the listed exchanges combined.

Over-the-Counter stocks are not limited to companies with penny stocks or newcomers to the corporate world. You can buy Coca Cola of Los Angeles, or Time, Inc., or Ozite, or many large railroads or public utilities in the Over-the-Counter market.

All mutual funds are traded Over-the-Counter. If you want to buy the stock of an insurance company or of a commercial bank, you will have to trade Over-the-Counter. Almost all government bonds, as well as municipal and authority bonds are traded OTC as are many corporate bonds, including those of some of the biggest companies.

To deal in Over-the-Counter transactions you do not need to hunt up a special dealer. Chances are your own broker has a trading department that handles his unlisted business. Some brokers will not require you to pay a net charge, but will trade in unlisted securities for your account on a commission basis.

There is no odd-lot charge for OTC stocks as there is for stocks traded on an exchange, because there are no requirements for round-lot deals on the Over-the-Counter transactions. Your dealer can sell as few or as many shares as you wish.

Penny stocks are the scourge of the regulatory officials of the Over-the-Counter marketplace. Unscrupulous dealers who trade exclusively in these cheap shares and operate from "bucket shops" or "boiler rooms" whose only assets are desks with telephones on them, are tracked down by the N.A.S.D. sooner or later, but frequently much damage has been done and many innocent people have been fleeced by the time justice is done.

Any company that is capitalized for more than three hundred thousand dollars, and which has more than twenty stockholders, has to register with the Securities and Exchange Commission. If its registration is approved, its stocks may be traded.

There is nothing to prevent one of the stockholders, even the major one, from trying to sell all or part of his stock. There is no valid reason why a dealer shouldn't undertake to sell it for him. In addition, the company may receive permission from its directors to sell some of its treasury stock, which can also reach the dealer and the marketplace.

Since these moves are made under the official scrutiny of the SEC and the N.A.S.D., they are legitimate and can in no way be construed as being harmful to potential stockholders. However, the value of a stock is not based on its legitimacy. It is compounded of many things, including proper capitalization, products, services and good management.

Quite often the stock of a corporation lacking all those things will reach the market and be particularly active for a while. Its price may be bid up under sales pressure. Such gains inevitably turn to losses when the selling effort ceases.

Low-priced stocks are selected for these excursions against the public's savings because buyers don't require large sums of money. You buy such stock more as an adventure—like playing the horses —than as an investment. Presumably you're not supposed to care too much if it turns out to be a bad venture for you.

This is not to say that you should avoid all low priced stocks. Many offer good opportunities, perhaps rare opportunities. These are the companies that will grow and prosper, because they have started out right and what they are doing is right.

There's one sure way to protect yourself, and that is to learn all about the company whose stock you're asked to purchase.

Subject it to the same measurements and qualifications you would if you were buying the highest-priced stock on the New York Stock Exchange. If you were to lay out several hundred or several thousand dollars for some stock certificates, you'd ask a lot of questions—the same questions posed in earlier chapters.

The con men who peddle low-value unlisted securities are assured a steady supply of customers by virtue of the same human weakness that serves all who play the "confidence game." It is human greed. If you don't lust for an easy dollar, a fast buck, you won't be so easily taken in by the peddlers of worthless stocks.

If you get a telephone call from some securities dealer, the best thing to do is to tell him that you have an account with a brokerage house and that you deal only there.

Be very skeptical about any securities offered you over the telephone by a salesman you do not know. Be wary of high-pressure sales.

Request that any information that is given to you on the phone be mailed to you at home, and specify that you want written information about the corporation, its operations, its profit picture, its management, its financial position, and its future prospects. Inform the salesman that you simply cannot buy any stock without having had a chance to thoroughly read and check such information.

When you get the printed information, take it to an expert for analysis. Your own reputable broker will do nicely.

Never—repeat, NEVER—be stampeded into buying stock by a salesman who tells you there is a specific time limit to get in at a certain price. If he knows a stock is going to be higher on a certain day, he's talking about a rigged market, and he won't be there to profit from it, for most likely he'll be in jail. More to the point, his firm will be suspended from trading.

You can use the Over-the-Counter market to exactly the same advantage that you derive from the New York Stock Exchange or any other exchange, if you take the same precautions that you should in buying any stock, anywhere.

The OTC market is the place to look for the "comers," the small companies that will grow and whose stock will be worth much more in the future. This is the place for wise speculation, but it takes a wily and knowledgable person to ferret out the right company.

This is probably a good place to mention also the American Stock Exchange, second largest in America, formerly known as the Curb Exchange.

The Curb Exchange was for years actually a curbstone market, located first on Wall and Hanover Streets and then later on Broad Street, in New York's financial district. It was one of the most colorful trading markets in the world, for all transactions were accomplished by hand signals, whistles and shouts from "floor traders" at curbside to brokers' representatives in the windows of the buildings adjoining the site. Even now, in its modern building on Broad Street, American Stock Exchange custom calls for floor traders to relay their orders by hand signals.

It is unfortunate that so many people regard the American Stock Exchange as a sort of training ground for the Big Board. It is true that a great many of the leading corporations now listed on the New York Stock Exchange got their "seasoning" on the Curb. Not so well recognized is the fact that a large number of America's foremost companies remain listed on the American Stock Exchange and apparently will remain there, without thought of moving up to the Big Board.

The listing requirements are a bit easier on the Curb than they are on the New York Stock Exchange, with the result that smaller companies can have their stock listed and traded there. As they grow richer and bigger, some remain, and some move on to the Big Board where stronger financial requirements prevail.

There is also in New York, the National Stock Exchange, a growing organization, where companies that are just a bit too small to qualify for the American Stock Exchange, have a chance to list their stocks for trading.

No smart investor ignores these smaller exchanges, particularly the American Stock Exchange where numerous senior companies are listed. And in the ranks of the smaller companies may be found the titans of tomorrow. Sometimes it is wiser to own, say, one-half of one percent of a company worth one million dollars than it is to own one-half of one percent of a company worth a hundred million. Aside from the fact that it would cost you a hundred times as much to own the same percentage in the larger company, you may be sacrificing the growth potential of the smaller company, the major ingredient in the rise in the price of a stock.

There are, in addition, eleven regional stock exchanges that are registered with the Securities and Exchange Commission, whose members are subject to rules and regulations governing their conduct in public trust.

The Midwest Stock Exchange in Chicago is the third largest exchange in the nation, and the largest regional exchange. Other regional exchanges include those in Boston, the Philadelphia-Baltimore-Washington exchange, Cincinnati, Detroit, Los Angeles, New Orleans, Pittsburgh, Salt Lake City, San Francisco and Spokane.

There are other exchanges in other cities, but they are not

registered with the Securities and Exchange Commission, hence do not in all instances impose the same rules and regulations on their members. They serve a useful purpose for local traders and dealers, and anyone buying stock on one of these un-registered exchanges, should do so through a local dealer. Mostly they are geared up to handle local commodities or strictly local enterprises, such as mining or exploration ventures.

The regional exchanges were organized originally to provide a marketplace for stocks of local publicly owned companies. As the companies grew and prospered they acquired nationwide reputations, and naturally they wanted their securities listed in New York, the heart of the financial center. A steady influx of new companies has kept the regional exchanges busy in recent years, even though there is constant attrition as the bigger companies take their listings to New York.

When a Big Board stock is traded on a regional exchange, the price is usually determined by the last price for the stock shown on the New York Stock Exchange ticker.

Not to be overlooked are the nearby Canadian exchanges, the highly-active Toronto Stock Exchange, and the prestigious Canadian Stock Exchange in Montreal. In addition there are important exchanges in Vancouver and Calgary, as well as the Curb Exchange in Montreal.

Because of the intensive activity in Canadian stocks during the 1950's, most American brokerage firms have correspondent firms in the Canadian cities, and there is a Canadian expert in every American brokerage house of consequence. These experts can guide you in the slight differences that exist in trading practices.

Canada's growth potential has by no means been realized, as every qualified economist who has studied the situation has testified, yet interest among American investors has cooled somewhat during the past few years. There is small doubt that it will be revived in the near future.

A large proportion of the stocks now listed on Canadian exchanges are on a dividend-paying basis, though the speculative companies still remain—those seeking minerals or oil, or engaged in pioneering enterprises. It was these, many of them mere penny stocks, that attracted so much American interest in the 1950's.

The Canadian government has tightened its laws, reducing the risk to investors, and has made its taxing policies more attractive, so that it may be expected that Canadian interest will perk up among American investors before long.

XXV *The Language of Wall Street*

There is nomenclature in the stock market, just as there is in anything else, and as a result, Wall Street has its special patois, a language that has evolved because it deals in specifics.

If a Wall Streeter talks of "flash prices," he is not referring to a Times Square neon display, but to a specific technique employed by the New York Stock Exchange when the ticker tape falls behind because of active trading.

Therefore, if you're going to buy common stocks and otherwise participate in the world of finance, you should familiarize yourself with the broad, most-used terms.

Noah Webster would never have approved the definitions that are listed below, and if Funk had presented them to Wagnalls, it would have sundered the partnership. But if you're going to be on the scrimmage line, you had better know what your teammates are talking about. There follows, then, a partial list of the most commonly used words and terms you'll hear around Wall Street, together with the broad and common definition of what they mean.

Account. That's what you have and maintain at your broker's office.

Account Executive. He's your registered representative or broker, or, to put it bluntly, the salesman who deals with you.

Accounts Payable and Receivable. In bookkeeping, these reveal what a company owes in current bills, and how much is owed to it.

Adjustment Bond. This is something for the amateur to avoid. It's a corporate bond whose interest is payable on a when, as and if basis. Good ones rank with Cumulative Preferred stock, but there are some that are not good.

American Stock Exchange. It's the second largest stock exchange in the nation, formerly known as the Curb Exchange.

Annuities. Insurance policies that pay a stipulated annual income for a specific period, or for the life of the beneficiary.

Annual Meeting. The once-a-year chance for stockholders either to approve or disapprove of their directors and management. Usually, however, the strength of your voice depends on how many shares you own. Directors are elected at this meeting.

Annual Report. This is where the chief executive officer explains what he has been doing all year and what he hopes to do next year. If necessary, he also tries to explain the harsh facts in the financial statements that accompany this report. It, like the Annual Meeting, is required by law.

Ask. It's what a seller is asking for his stock, usually in Over-the-Counter transactions. You make a bid. He does the asking. When bid and asked get together, there's a sale.

Assets. Come on, now—you know what those are. They are a total of all the cash, the receivables, the inventory, the machinery, the bricks and mortar, the real estate and the good will of what a company owns.

Auction. That's the market in which stocks are traded. An "auction market" is maintained by the New York Stock Exchange or the American Stock Exchange.

Averages. The prices of selected stocks, weighted and averaged out, designed to give you a general idea of how the market is doing, whether it's up or down. The most common is the Industrial Average compiled by Dow-Jones & Company. It's called "The Dow." Also important to traders is the Standard & Poor's average. The *New York Times* also has an average. So does the Associated Press.

Averaging (Dollar Cost Averaging). The act of spending a specific amount of money at specified intervals to buy a certain stock. This way you buy more stock when the price is lower, and less stock when it is higher.

Balance Sheet. The all-revealing soul of the Annual Report.

Learn to read it. It gives you an accurate picture of the status of a company. Read this before you read what the chief executive officer has to say about the future.

Balanced Funds. Mutual funds that are supposed to be invested on a broad spectrum so that if there is a recession in one segment of the list, there will be prosperity and high prices in another.

Bear Market. When stock prices sell lower for a period of three months or more.

Bid. Your offer to buy a stock.

Big Board. It's the New York Stock Exchange, at 11 Wall Street.

Blocks. Large sales of stock, usually by banks, insurance companies or the institutions in units of one hundred shares.

Blue Sky Laws. The regulations of the Securities and Exchange Commission governing the filing and registration of a new offering of stock. They are designed to eliminate any exaggeration, and are so-named because in the old days, some entrepreneurs used to promise the blue sky.

Bonds. Notes issued by a company to a lender, pledging to pay a specific rate of interest and to redeem the bond—or pay back the note—at a specified time. There is a wide variety of bonds.

Book Value. It's what a stock would be worth on a per share basis if a corporation should be liquidated at fair market prices.

Broker's Letter. An advisory telling customers what the experts think of the condition of the market, or an analysis of a special stock, group of stocks, or industry.

Bucket Shop. A broker who accepts your order to buy a stock, accepts your money, and then doesn't buy the stock, hoping he can get it for you later at a lower price, and at a profit to himself. This is illegal, but you'll hear the term.

Bull Market. When prices of a majority of stocks tend to rise over a period of three months or longer.

Call. A request from your broker to put up more margin—to increase the size of your downpayment on a margin loan.

Call (as in Put and Call). A contract giving you the right to buy one hundred shares of stock at a specified price within a certain time.

Capital Gain. You'd better learn all about this one. A capital gain is the profit realized on the sale or purchase of a security if it is held more than six months.

Capitalization. The amount of venture capital put into a corporation by its owners (or stockholders). Not to be confused with Net Worth.

Classified Stock. Stock issued in different classes, e.g., "Class A" or "Class B," and usually carrying some restriction.

Closed-End Fund. An Investment Trust whose capitalization is created at the outset and is kept constant.

Commissions. You won't have to learn about these, for your broker will tell you. It's what he gets for handling your order.

Common Stock. A share of a company's ownership, representing your capital investment, with no restrictions and no special privileges.

Convertible Bond. A bond representing a loan to a company which may be converted to common stock in lieu or repayment or redemption.

Cumulative Preferred. Stock that takes precedence on dividends. If a company cannot pay dividends on its common stock, the dividend on the preferred stock accumulates until such time as it can be paid. The accumulated dividends must be paid to the preferred stockholders before any dividends can be paid to the owners of common stock.

Curb Exchange. Former name of the present American Stock Exchange.

Customers' Man. A Registered Representative or stock broker.

Cyclical Stock. Stock whose earnings are affected by changes in the seasons or by the business cycles. The ambition of the conglomerates is to eliminate cycles.

Debenture. A bond that is backed only by the general credit of the corporation. In reality, it's an unsecured loan.

Disclosure. One of the toughest requirements of the Securities and Exchange Commission is that one called *Full Disclosure*, which mandates that no corporation may give any information affecting its stock to any one person without simultaneously making the information known to the entire investing public.

Discounting. The knack of anticipating things in advance, so that events, when they occur, have been "discounted."

Equity. The amount of a company's capital represented by a share of common stock.

Equity Capital. Another name for Venture Capital. It's the money raised for a company by selling its stock to the public.

Ex-Dividend. It's what happens to a stock on the record date for payment of a dividend. Dividends are declared payable on a certain date to holders of *record* on a specific date. Four days before that record date a stock goes "ex-dividend," and often sells for a price that is lower by the amount of the dividend. That's because it takes four days to deliver stock.

Flash Prices. Prices of selected leading stocks "flashed" onto the tape to give a report of how the market is doing, when the ticker lags under heavy trading.

Floor Reporters. Employees of the stock exchange who monitor trades at trading posts and post price changes as they occur.

Floor Traders. These are men who own membership in the New York Stock Exchange and who buy and sell only for their own accounts.

Formula Investing. Maintaining a balance in the portfolio between stocks and bonds, according to a specific ratio determined by the formula. Its object is prudence and safety.

Growth Stocks. The securities in certain industries and specific companies that seem likely to grow rapidly during the period ahead.

Hypothecate. To pledge stock for a loan, a process used commonly in margin accounts and in selling short.

Inside Price. The price at which an Over-the-Counter broker will sell his stock to another broker.

Institutional Investor. The manager of the portfolio of a large fund or trust.

Investment Bankers. Institutions that specialize in raising equity or venture capital for long term investment in corporate enterprises.

Investment Club. Groups of people who contribute regularly to a fund to buy securities. These clubs are formed in neighborhoods, lodges and associations.

Investment Companies. Another name for closed-end investment trusts.

Loading Charge. The fee, or, the percentage, charged as commission by the seller of a Mutual Fund.

Long. The opposite of selling short. A bull, optimistic about the future of the market, goes *long*, by buying stock.

Margin. The downpayment that you make when buying stock on credit.

M.I.P. The Monthly Investment Plan, that allows you to invest a certain amount each month (or quarter) to buy a pre-determined stock.

Municipals. The tax-free bonds of municipalities and authorities.

Mutual Fund. An open-ended investment company that invests in the securities of corporations and in government bonds, and sells shares of itself to the public.

Odd Lot. Less than a hundred shares, which is a block, or a round lot. There are Odd Lot brokers who specialize in handling these smaller sales.

Option. Both a put and a call are known as options, since the owner has the right to exercise an option as to whether he wishes to buy or sell.

Outside Price. The price at which an Over-the-Counter broker will sell stock to a customer.

Over-the-Counter. Trading in an unlisted security, one not listed on an exchange.

Paper Profit. What you have if a stock increases in value and you don't sell it.

Par Value. The equity value or capitalization value of each share of a company's stock. It doesn't mean much to you if the company has been in business for very long.

Participating Preferred. Stock that earns guaranteed dividends, and also participates in any extra profits earned by a company.

Pools. Uh-uh. Don't touch. They're illegal. It's not right to join together with rich speculators to manipulate the market.

Price-Earnings-Ratio. A once-useful measurement for seeing if a stock was overpriced. A good ratio was formerly ten-to-one, that is if a company earned ten dollars a share, its stock should sell in the neighborhood of one dollar a share. Forget it—today it rarely counts.

Private Placement. When a new issue of stock is sold in its entirety to private interests.

Public Offering. Just the opposite of the above.

Pyramiding. The art of buying more stock on margin by collateralizing the paper profits of that stock that you own. A practice of the 1920's frowned upon the the SEC today.

Quote Board. The focal point in every brokerage office of any size, where current prices of stocks are posted.

Registered Representative. The broker or salesman or customers' man who handles your brokerage account.

Right. A right or *Warrant* entitles you to purchase stock at a specified time for a specific price.

Risk Capital. Euphemistically called "Equity Capital." It's the money that investors put into the capitalization of a corporation.

Round Lot. A block of a hundred shares of stock traded on the New York Stock Exchange.

Seat. The term used for membership of the New York Stock Exchange or American Stock Exchange. It originally applied only to N.Y.S.E. when members actually did have seats or chairs, where they sat and oversaw proceedings.

Secondary. This results when an offering of stock does not sell well the first time it is put on the market, and its underwriters are forced to buy it back to stabilize the market. They hold it until the market improves and re-offer it as a "secondary offering."

Securities and Exchange Commission. The Federal agency that regulates and polices the exchanges, the marketplace, and those who do business there.

Short Interest. A monthly report by the New York Stock Exchange of the total number of shares on which sellers are selling short.

Specialist. The broker, on the floor of the stock exchange, standing at a particular trading post, who executes the order that you have placed with your broker. He "keeps the book," and tries to stabilize prices to prevent rapid price changes.

Split. Re-issue of stock certificates on the basis of multiples (e.g., two shares of new stock for one share of the old) usually as a result of the high price of the old share.

Stock Dividend. The distribution of previously unissued shares of stock in lieu of a cash dividend.

Stop-Loss-Order. An order to sell stock at a certain price to prevent further losses.

Straddle. The purchase of a put and a call at current market price. A *Spread* is the purchase of a put and a call simultaneously at different prices.

Tape. The high-speed ticker tape that relays stock prices as they are set on the floor of the stock exchange to brokerage offices throughout the country.

Two-Dollar Broker. The substitute broker who actually executes an order when the regular broker is busy on other orders. He actually gets more than two dollars—the name is a holdover from the old days.

Warrant. The same as a *Right,* or almost the same. It permits you to buy stock at a specific price at a certain time.

Wash Sale. The simultaneous purchase and sale of large blocks of stock, done solely to generate public interest in all of the activity in the stock. Now illegal.

Watered Stock. Selling stock of inflated value to the unsuspecting public. No longer possible under SEC rules and supervision.

Wire House. A broker who maintains branch offices or correspondents in several other cities, linked together by teletype and telephone lines.

Working Capital. In the Annual Report or latest interim report of a company, the difference between net current assets and net current liabilities is Working Capital, or the amount of money available to run the business.